Young Children's Social Emotional Learning

Young Children's Social Emotional Learning: The COPE-Resilience Program is a manual that is designed to support early childhood educators in the delivery of the COPE Resilience (COPE-R) program, an evidence-based program designed to teach empathy, resilience, and prosocial skills to children.

Grounded in extensive research and experience in psychology and early childhood, the program is built on a series of activities that help children develop their capacity for emotional understanding, caring for others, open communication, polite and respectful behaviours, and empathic sharing. The manual includes:

- Theoretical concepts underpinning COPE-R such as self-regulation, emotional intelligence, positive psychology, coping, resilience, and wellbeing in early childhood education.
- A "How-To" section to guide readers in the implementation of COPE-R.
- Over 40 activities templates (including examples of teachers' adaptations) with easy-to-navigate icon legends.
- Facilitator notes on and considerations for working with younger children and children of diverse backgrounds.
- Teaching tips for each topic area and a feature piece on the insights from an early childhood teacher who is experienced in implementing COPE-R.
- Supplementary materials, including a set of situation and coping images.

Each activity includes directions for children as well as guidelines for educators, and is designed to be used flexibly in various early learning contexts, enabling educators to select activities that best suit their setting.

Erica Frydenberg is Associate Professor in Psychology, Melbourne Graduate School of Education, University of Melbourne, Australia.

Janice Deans is Associate Director, Early Childhood Education, University of Melbourne, Australia.

Rachel Liang is Honorary Research Fellow, Melbourne Graduate School of Education, University of Melbourne, Australia.

Young Children's Social Emotional Learning

The COPE-Resilience Program

Erica Frydenberg, Janice Deans, and Rachel Liang

LONDON AND NEW YORK

First published 2021
by Routledge
2 Park Square, Milton Park, Abingdon, Oxon OX14 4RN

and by Routledge
52 Vanderbilt Avenue, New York, NY 10017

Routledge is an imprint of the Taylor & Francis Group, an informa business

© 2021 Erica Frydenberg, Janice Deans, and Rachel Liang

The right of Erica Frydenberg, Janice Deans, and Rachel Liang to be identified as authors of this work has been asserted by them in accordance with sections 77 and 78 of the Copyright, Designs and Patents Act 1988.

All rights reserved. No part of this book may be reprinted or reproduced or utilised in any form or by any electronic, mechanical, or other means, now known or hereafter invented, including photocopying and recording, or in any information storage or retrieval system, without permission in writing from the publishers.

Trademark notice: Product or corporate names may be trademarks or registered trademarks, and are used only for identification and explanation without intent to infringe.

British Library Cataloguing-in-Publication Data
A catalogue record for this book is available from the British Library

Library of Congress Cataloging-in-Publication Data
A catalog record has been requested for this book

ISBN: 978-0-367-89588-4 (hbk)
ISBN: 978-0-367-89589-1 (pbk)
ISBN: 978-1-003-01996-1 (ebk)

Typeset in Bembo
by River Editorial Ltd, Devon, UK

Contents

List of figures vii

Acknowledgements viii

Note from the authors ix

PART 1
Foundations of COPE-R   1

Theoretical concepts underpinning COPE-R   2

Theory of Cognitive Development 2
Socio-Cultural Theory of Development 3
Ecological Systems Theory 3

Other theoretical concepts   6

Attachment theory 6
Self-regulation 6
Emotional intelligence 6
Positive psychology 7
Positive education in the pre-school years 7

Overview of the coping research   9

The relationships between coping and resilience 9
Early Years Coping Cards 9
Resilience 9

An outline of COPE-R   11

Program background 11
Introduction 11
Aims of the program 11

Theoretical basis for each of the topic areas in COPE-R   12

Foundational emotion understanding 12
Caring/kindness 12
Open communication 12
Politeness 13
Empathic sharing 13
Development of the program 13
Taiwanese adaptation 14

Contents

PART 2
Implementation of COPE-R   15

An overview of Part 2   16

  i **Program in brief**   17

  ii **Icon legends**   18

  iii **Important considerations for educators/facilitators**   19

Create a safe and nurturing environment 19
Be a good "empathy" role model for children 19
Encourage children to practise their skills during the day 20
Use positive reinforcement for appropriate behaviours 20
Holding children's attention 20
Working with children with trauma 21

  iv **Program activities**   22

  v **A teacher's experience and reflection on COPE-R**   94

  vi **Supplementary materials for educators/facilitators/teachers**   95

Program background references   *96*

Appendix 1: Mindfulness and relaxation   *99*

Appendix 2: Situation and coping images for personal use   *101*

Index   *104*

Figures

Part 1

1 An integration of cognitive, ecological system and socio-cultural theories of development — 4

Part 2

2 Finding Feelings — 26
3 Clay Feelings — 31
4 The Moon Poem — 34
5 Composing music — 37
6 Children's version of a feeling thermometer — 38
7 Getting Hurt Situation Card — 43
8 Children's discussion on the "Getting Hurt" Situation card — 44
9 Caring for all living creatures — 50
10 Caring for family — 51
11 Caring for the world — 52
12 "Wanting to Play with Others" Situation Card — 57
13 Listening with the whole body — 59
14 A good listener — 59
15 Bullied Situation Card — 64
16 "Choosing a Group to Play With" Situation Card — 73
17 Mandala of silence — 90
18 Children creating a silence mandala — 91

Acknowledgements

The COPE-R program has been developed and introduced at the Early Learning Centre at the University of Melbourne. It has been one of the many aspects of the social emotional learning curriculum that has been implemented over the past six years. The implementation has resulted in ongoing evaluation and improvements. We have learned a lot, as have the children, teachers, and parents. It also means that there are so many contributors to acknowledge and thank.

Firstly, the staff of the Early Learning Centre at the University of Melbourne under the leadership of Dr Jan Deans, who have made the program and the insights from its multiple iterations possible. One lead teacher, Suzana Klarin, has been there throughout the journey. She has contributed to the program, its development, and learnings. She has shared her experience and wisdom, not only with the children, their families, and her colleagues, but most generously with the scholarly academic community and beyond. Her experience and insights are quoted extensively throughout this publication.

There are numerous researchers and developers who have contributed to this manuscript, including the earliest researchers who conceptualised coping in the early years, such as those who developed the first iteration of the COPE-R program, Neisha Kiernan, Danielle Kaufman, Chelsea Cornell, and Prishni Dobee.

Since the time of the first application numerous researchers and developers have contributed to the program, including those associated with evaluations and understanding of the constructs, namely Kirsten Chalmers, Kelly Yeo, Haruka Tsurutani, Dominique Pang, Lying Su, and Esmerelda Lambe. In more recent years Monique Alexander has continued to research the program, and Gavin Duarte has provided extensive quotes from his interview with a lead teacher, particularly those reflecting on a teacher's experience in Section V of Part 2 of this manual. Marissa Wu has completed substantive research and has taken the program to Taiwan and considered issues associated with adaptation in a culturally different context.

The work of all researchers and teachers is gratefully acknowledged. One teacher, Suzana Klarin, has been committed to the COPE-R project from the outset and her contribution shines throughout the volume.

Note from the authors

Since the 1960s coping research has provided a valuable platform from which to advance human endeavour and adaptation. In COPE-Resilience program we incorporate values training in the early years. As we submit this manuscript, we are living through the COVID-19 pandemic. There is a realisation that it is time to reset and look at our values, the principles by which we live. There is no better place to start than with educators of young children as they lead them through the early years. At this time in world history there is an urgent requirement for teachers to support children's understandings of what it means to care for and respect others and the environment, and to learn that empathy and sensitivity are essential human qualities to ensure a peaceful and harmonious world.

1 Foundations of COPE-R

2 Foundations of COPE-R

Theoretical concepts underpinning COPE-R

The COPE-Resilience program is grounded in the knowledge and belief that children's development is a dynamic and complex process which is best understood in context. Among the myriad of theories that help to explore and explain different aspects of child development, this book draws on three prominent theories which still have an important influence on our contemporary understanding of how children grow, learn, and change. We will first introduce the earlier works of Jean Piaget (1952) on cognitive development and of Lev Vygotsky (1962) on the social and cultural origins of development. Then we will revisit the work of Uri Bronfenbrenner's (1979) Ecological Systems Theory, which has been widely adopted and adapted since the 1970s to explain development in context. An integration of these three theories is illustrated in Figure 1 to assist with understanding how children are influenced by their social-cultural contexts as they progress flexibly through the developmental stages.

Theory of Cognitive Development

Piaget (1952) viewed children as active learners, a view in which their development and knowledge are based on their experiences and interactions with the world. The child actively constructs their understanding of their world through exploring and interacting with the environment. These understandings form a set of mental representations of the world, which he called schema, that the child uses both to understand and to respond to situations. In addition to perceiving children as active learners, he proposed four discrete stages of child development, with each stage explaining the processes and mechanisms employed to assist the development of the child's cognitive skills by building more numerous and elaborate schemas.

These four stages of cognitive development, with an indication of the age at which the average child would reach each stage, include:

- *Sensorimotor (birth–2 years old)*: The infant learns about the environment through responding to sensory stimuli through motor actions. The child acquires knowledge and understanding through physically interacting with the object (e.g., looking, touching, grabbing).
- *Pre-Operational (2–7 years old)*: Children begin to understand symbolic meaning as opposed to the physical and concrete observations made in the previous stage. During this stage, children begin to use symbols in a more organised and logical manner.
- *Concrete Operational (7–11 years old)*: Children's thinking becomes more flexible and logical. While children's learning mainly stems from actions, their ability to think in more abstract ways increases. This stage marks the understanding that quantities remain the same even if they change in shape or are different in appearance.
- *Formal Operations (11–15 years old)*: The child/adolescent gains the ability to think hypothetically and uses abstract ideas, resulting in a more effective manner of thinking. Adolescents begin to have conversations about abstract topics in a meaningful manner.

According to Piaget (1952), each child goes through the stages in the same order through processes of assimilation (i.e., modifying new information to fit existing schema), accommodation (i.e., restructuring schemas so that the new information can fit in better), and (dis)equilibration (i.e., a state of mental (im)balance). Children's ability to learn is determined by biological maturation, which allows adults to interact with children in an appropriate manner related to their cognitive developmental ability. The key implication of Piaget's theory of education and learning is that teachers should create an environment that facilitates active exploration and learning by discovery for the children rather than direct tuition.

However, Piaget's theory underestimated young children's ability in some areas and his theory did not take into account the role that culture and education play in promoting cognitive development. Other theorists see a more flexible progression by children through their developmental stages that is linked to socio-cultural context, where children's higher order of thinking can be promoted through modelling and observation as well as through first-hand experience.

Socio-Cultural Theory of Development

Vygotsky (1962) laid the groundwork for the "Socio-Cultural Theory of Development", which emphasises the social and cultural origins of development. Vygotsky considered social process such as interacting with parents, caregivers, peers and the culture forms the basis for children's learning. The essential role of social interactions in learning means cognitive and linguistic development can differ between cultures. Vygotsky believed in the powerful role of language acquisition in shaping children's thoughts and growing cognitive capabilities. He suggested children's first utterances with peers or adults are for the purpose of communication. These utterances then become private speech, i.e., how children talk to themselves while carrying out a difficult cognitive task, and once mastered children develop internalised "inner speech" as they become more capable of working on their own without help from a caregiver or parent. It is theorised that inner speech allows the development of more advanced cognitive abilities such as executive functioning.[1]

Additionally, the concept of the zone of proximal development (ZPD) places emphasis on social interactions such as adult guidance and peer collaboration to support children to "stretch" their level of skills and knowledge development in accomplishing tasks that they cannot yet understand or perform on their own. The adult's and the child's interactions through scaffolding (targeted assistance) have also been shown to have significant influences on the child's learning by progressively extending the ZPD. The key implication of this theory for parents and educators is that, by providing children with experiences which are in their ZPD, they can encourage and advance children's learning and understanding of the world and the community in which they are embedded.

Ecological Systems Theory

Throughout the late 1970s and 1980s, Bronfenbrenner (1979) proposed the model "Ecological Systems Theory", which views human development as an interaction between the individual and their environment. The model arose due to a lack of focus

---

[1] Executive functioning is a group of the mental processes that enable us to plan, focus attention, remember instructions, and manage multiple tasks at the same time (Center on the Developing Child, 2020).

around the role of context on development in theories of human development up until that time.

The five ecological systems for child development described by Bronfenbrenner include:

1. *Microsystem*: The small, immediate environment within which the child lives and interacts, such as family, caregivers, their school and day care centre.
2. *Mesosystem*: The interactions between different parts of a child's microsystem, e.g., between parents and the school; between parents and peers.
3. *Exosystem*: The people and organisations that indirectly affect the child, e.g., parents' workplace arrangements, the neighbourhood, etc.
4. *Macrosystem*: The largest and the outermost layer of the context within which a child is embedded, but which still has a great impact on a child's development. This includes the economy, societal beliefs, cultural values, governance of laws, and freedom.
5. *Chronosystem*: How a person and his/her environment changes over the life course, as well as socio-historical circumstances, such as growing economic equalities.

In the mid-1980s, in response to research starting to over-emphasise context and ignore development, Bronfenbrenner (1994) presented his "Bioecological Systems Theory".

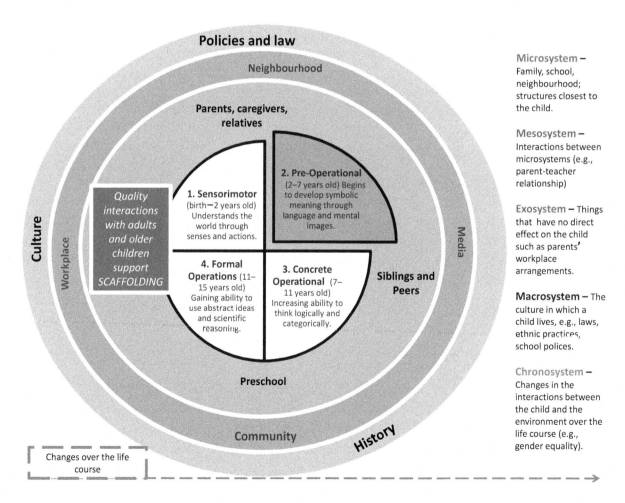

Figure 1 An integration of cognitive, ecological system and socio-cultural theories of development.

This theory is based on the Process-Person-Context-Time (PPCT) model:

- *Process*: Proximal processes or the interaction between a person and their environment as the primary mechanism for development.
- *Person*: The role that the individual and their personal characteristics (e.g., age, sex, gender, physical or mental health) plays on social interactions with their environment and consequently their proximal processes.
- Context: The five ecological systems (as above) that serve as the context for an individual's development.
- Time: The influence that micro-time (events during the proximal processes), meso-time (extent of the processes, e.g., a few days or weeks or years) and macro-time (the chronosystem) have on a child's development.

The bioecological systems model adds to our understanding of human development by highlighting how both the person and the environment influence one another bidirectionally, and the implications for early years research, practice, and polices.

Other theoretical concepts

Attachment theory

Attachment theory reflects the deep bonds that connect persons to one another across time and place. The early proponent of attachment theory, Bowlby (1969), emphasised the importance of the relation between infants and their caregivers, particularly parents. Bowlby focused on the relationship between infants and their mothers in terms of social emotional and cognitive development. In recent times, attachment theory has encompassed the relationships developed throughout the lifespan, often expressed in terms of belonging (Frydenberg, Deans & O'Brien, 2012). The critical period for developing attachments is 0–5 years. Hence the pre-school years provide an important opportunity to build on those early relationships and prepare children for the school years. The skills of attachment and belonging include communication and language skills, which underscore the COPE-R program. Programs such as COPE-R have emotion knowledge and practices and include self-regulatory processes. By exploring empathy and sharing and caring, children learn to relate to others, including peers. While attachment is determined by a host of temperamental factors, including having an engaging predisposition, the interactions in the pre-school setting provide opportunities for life-skill development.

Self-regulation

Marc Brackett, the author of *Permission to Feel* (Brackett, 2019) and the RULER program (Brackett, Rivers, Reyes & Salovey, 2012), devotes his theory to the development of emotions and how we recognise, understand, label, express, and regulate them. Emotions are at the core of our being and influence all our actions and reactions. In infancy it is about the need for comfort and release from discomfort, but beyond that it is about how emotions influence our relationships with others and our perceptions of the world. While control or regulation of emotions is the most challenging of the RULER skills it is teachable, but it is dependent on the four previously learnt skills. In COPE-R we emphasise the recognition, understanding, labelling, and expression of emotions in age-appropriate ways, from which the development of self-regulation follows. Adults, such as parents and teachers, are core influencers, along with peers, hence the way each of us regulates our emotions to be the best calm selves that will influence young children. Brackett encourages us to use the meta-moment, to stop and draw breath before responding, while other programs describe it as "stop, think and do" (Petersen & Adderley, 2002).

Emotional intelligence

The concept of emotional intelligence or EI has been popularised since the mid-1990s by Daniel Goleman in his book *Emotional Intelligence* (2005), first published in 1995. Some years earlier Salovey and Mayer described EI as "the ability to monitor one's own and others' emotions, to discriminate among them, and to use the information to guide one's thinking and actions" (Salovey & Mayer, 1990, p.189). That is, emotions can be both recognised in oneself and in others, using cues that are both verbal and nonverbal. Being able to regulate or manage emotions has been an important feature of EI and is closely linked to wellbeing (Mayer, Roberts & Barsade, 2008; Mayer & Salovey, 1993). Another aspect of EI is the ability to interact well with others, utilising emotional understandings and putting this information to work in daily interactions and communications. This is commonly referred as social intelligence, which is highly linked to success in relationships and life in general. Social skills can be nurtured and improved from the pre-school years, which contribute to early school success (Denham, Bassett & Miller, 2017). As with general intelligence some people are inherently more intelligent than others and the same is the case with EI. The important difference is that EI can be developed, the earlier the better. While much of the popular writing has been in the adult domain it is readily acknowledged that the teaching of EI and the associated skills provides a significant opportunity in the early years, a time when cognition and language development occur at such a rapid pace.

EI has often been considered to be anything that is not IQ. However, there is real science behind EI and "there is intelligence behind emotions" according to Brackett and his colleagues (Brackett et al., 2012). Brackett developed the RULER program, with the acronym standing for recognition, understanding, labelling, expression, and regulation of emotions. The acronym covers all the elements that are important in EI. The emphasis in RULER, as in COPE-R, is that there are cognitions (thoughts) and affect (feelings), and the two are interdependent. How we think affects how we feel and how we feel affects how we think. An additional element is that, if we can name it, we can "tame" it. Therefore, there is an emphasis on labelling emotions and subsequently developing the skills to manage them both in order to enhance and to regulate them. EI can be developed and cultivated in the early years by teaching children to first become aware, take notice and have the language to label emotions (Bailey et al., 2019). Emotional literacy is a core element of COPE-R, as it is of RULER. Emotions are not inherently good or bad; it is about knowing when and how to utilise or regulate them. For example, feeling joy can be appropriate when something good has happened, such as receiving a gift, but not when someone is hurt. Alternatively, anger or frustration may be appropriate when one is being teased but not when receiving a gift. It is both what one thinks and how these emotions are expressed that matters, and that is coping.

Positive psychology

At a child level, positive psychology is about bringing up children who are engaged with the world around them, who retain curiosity to explore their environment, and who gain satisfaction when they accomplish a task. We want children not only to be willing to engage in challenging activities but also to be able to engage with and relate to others, to show gratitude, and to appreciate their surroundings. While positive psychology emphasises the important experience of positive emotions, it does not imply that we are not interested in also identifying and labelling negative emotions. We learn to appreciate the good through negative experiences and losses. However, generally it is through positive emotional experiences that we broaden and build our personal resources for living the good life.

Positive Education in the pre-school years

Positive Education as defined by Seligman and colleagues (2009) is an education for both traditional skills and for happiness. It aims to address the gap between what we all want for our children – happiness, and positive physical and mental health – versus the traditional focus on academic achievement as a measure of success in school. It is not a focus on mental health instead of academic achievement, but is rather a focus on mental health in order to set the stage and give students the opportunity for learning. Optimal learning is thus holistic, progressing simultaneously in areas of health, cognition, personal and social development, and wellbeing.

Within the educational context, schools are increasingly urged to provide students with opportunities to not only grow academically, but also to become caring, responsible, and productive members of society (White & Waters, 2015). A key aspect of achieving this in the early years is through teaching valuable life skills that assist early years learners to strengthen their relationships, build positive emotions, enhance personal resilience, promote mindfulness, and encourage a healthy lifestyle (Frydenberg, Deans & Liang, 2020). A focus on holistic wellbeing as one of the major learning outcomes for the early years education can offer children a strong foundation on which they can build a successful life as caring, responsible, and productive members of society into the future.

Overview of the coping research

The relationships between coping and resilience

Coping comprises the thoughts, feelings, and actions that we employ to deal with the demands of situations. There are many aspects to coping and different individuals may react to a situation in different ways, such as using helpful coping and unhelpful coping strategies. Children learn helpful coping skills through modelling by adults, and through interactions with adults and children. In the educational context, this can be achieved through intentional teaching and the use of visual tools such as the Early Years Coping Cards (Frydenberg & Deans, 2011), role-plays, and games that depict issues of concern to children and how they might deal with them.

Early Years Coping Cards

Research on early years coping has indicated that young children can identify the situations that they find challenging or difficult to manage, and that they can also identify a wide range of both productive and non-productive coping strategies for different contexts such as school and family (Frydenberg et al., 2020). Conversations with young children can be facilitated with the use of visual prompts such as the Early Years Coping Cards (Frydenberg & Deans, 2011). The Early Years Coping Cards comprise a set of "Situation Cards" that depict the following situations: "losing something or someone special", "saying goodbye to someone you love", "being in trouble with an adult", "scared of the dark", "afraid of trying something new", "being teased or bullied", "being left out by your friends", "broken toy", and "getting hurt". The set of Coping Cards is made up of images that depict both productive and non-productive coping strategies. The productive coping strategies include: "think happy thoughts", "hug a toy", "play", "help others", "talk to an adult", and "work hard". The non-productive coping strategies include: "worry", "run away", "hide", "scream", "complain of pain", "keep feelings to self", and "blame yourself". This visual resource is designed specifically to stimulate conversations between adults and children on a range of situations that children aged 4–8 years have identified as challenging and difficult to manage.

At school or at home, adults can have conversations with children about challenging situations and possible coping strategies to model proactive and productive coping behaviour. Cards depicting situations and coping images can be used in multiple ways and there is no right or wrong way to use them. It is up to the creativity of each individual user to adapt their use of the cards to the specific situation, and this might mean that only one situation and numerous coping images are used at any one time.

Resilience

Resilience refers to the ability to be able to bounce back despite adversity or setbacks. Having good coping resources contributes to resilience. It is an asset that can be acquired through teaching and practice (Frydenberg, 2017).

Since the early years of coping research when theorists articulated and operationalised the coping construct as being namely thoughts, feelings, and actions, there have been adaptations of the adult theorising to that of children and adolescents. We know that children sometimes respond to threatening or challenging situations with fear or anxiety.

Foundations of COPE-R

Coping is the response of the individual to the situations that they encounter and how they appraise those situations as being one of harm or challenge. After the initial appraisal of the situation they would then ask the question, "do I have the strategies to cope"? It is these coping resources that we want to build up through exposure to experience and teaching. Indeed, the learning environment is one where we scaffold and support children to explore and try out new things. Intrinsically there is no right or wrong coping – it is the situation that determines which is the right strategy to be used. Coping has been construed as being akin to adaptation. There are helpful and unhelpful coping strategies, depending on the situation and the outcome. For example, a young child fearing the dark may call out to the parent to get them to comfort them – that is, to seek assistance, or just cry themselves to sleep and refuse to go to bed willingly when tired. Coping strategies are accumulated to become part of an individual's coping habit or repertoire. Both helpful and unhelpful coping strategies can operate that way. Through the use of helpful coping strategies children can also build confidence in the knowledge that they have the resources to cope (Frydenberg, 2015). While coping is a process of the accumulation of practices, resilience is an outcome. Thus, in COPE-R we teach the language of coping through age-appropriate visual tools and have conversations about thoughts and feelings in order to build up a language of coping and a collection of helpful coping habits.

An outline of COPE-R

Program background

This section provides detailed information about the aims of the program, its theoretical foundations, and its development. The goals of the program are addressed by using evidence-based activities grounded in the following theoretical research. There are also recommendations to guide you in delivering the program.

Introduction

This is a program designed to teach empathy and prosocial skills to children aged 4–8 years in the context of early childhood development guidelines in numerous jurisdictions. For example, in the United Kingdom, the United States, and Australia there are similarities and differences across the three communities both in labelling the social and emotional skill areas and in how the areas are described. Issues around self-awareness, self-management, and relationships management appear in each of the settings with variations on emphasis and focus. Additionally, empathy and caring for others feature to some extent, as does responsible decision making (Frydenberg, Deans & Liang, 2020). Social emotional competencies have been incorporated into various curricula with a focus on relationship building, belonging, and community, and the skills required to support these objectives. Areas covered in this program include understanding emotions, caring for others, open communication, polite/respectful behaviours, empathic sharing, and a review of these key topics. These topics are taught using discussions and activities and are designed to be implemented in the classroom or in small groups.

> "We realised this is the first time [after COPE-R] that even the youngest children will be socially and emotionally ready for school."

Aims of the program

The program aims to:

- Develop children's knowledge and skills in recognising their own and other's feelings and emotions.
- Encourage children's ability to be resilient through use of positive coping strategies.
- Increase children's knowledge and use of prosocial and empathic behaviours towards each other such as caring and sharing.
- Enhance children's empathy towards the environment, animals, and diverse peoples.

Theoretical basis for each of the topic areas in COPE-R

Foundational emotion understanding

A comprehensive body of emotion language is helpful as a communication tool to advance social emotional learning (Brackett, 2019; Deans, Klarin, Liang & Frydenberg, 2017; Pang, Frydenberg, Liang & Deans, 2018). Children as young as three have emotional understanding (EU), which is associated with recognising and understanding one's own and other's emotions. The way in which children read, interpret, express, and understand various emotions are guided and affected by the expectations and rules of the culture and community in which they live (Ma, Tamir & Miyamoto, 2017).

EU is underpinned by the theory of the mind (ToM) that posits that pre-school children can appreciate inner states and can distinguish between true or false belief systems. EU in turn is considered to increase with prosocial behaviours such as helping and sharing (Eisenberg, Fabes & Spinrad, 2006; Ornaghi, Pepe & Grazzani, 2016),

Caring/kindness

Caring can be described as empathy in action. Early childhood educators in Nordic countries base their work on caring, creating an affirming and nurturing ethos (Fugelsnes, 2018). The underlying premise is that there is a reciprocal relation between children and adults, and as adults model these behaviours social learning takes place.

The establishment of empathetic behaviours is important for moral reasoning and overall prosocial behaviour (Decety, 2011; Feshbach & Feshbach, 2009). Baron-Cohen & Wheelwright (2004) distinguish the cognitive from the emotional dimension of empathy (Frydenberg et al., 2012). Going beyond the saying "I'm sorry" requires children to have an internal voice that tells them to act with kindness, consideration, respect, and fairness, often called the emergence of conscience (Smith, 2013). The foundations of conscience are compassion, sympathy, and empathy. And this is an intellectual experience that is accessible to 4-year-olds. It fits into the social emotional curriculum well.

Open communication

The ability to communicate is an essential life skill for all children in the 21st century and becomes of increasing importance as children proceed through the school years. The universal communication skills include listening, being able to be assertive, and problem-solving. Each are life skills that are common across the age groups and are taught both to parents and teachers as well as children (Frydenberg, 2015).[2]

Research shows that improved communication skills lead to better outcomes in learning, behaviour, and confidence (Bain, James & Harrison, 2015). Much of classroom practice incorporates communication skills through the classroom environment, where there are displays of children's work that can elicit discussion, stories that elicit discussion, activity tables where children collaborate and talk while working on their activities, and so on. But what the researchers also highlight is the value and importance of engaging parents in open communication when they bring the children to

---

2 Frydenberg, E. (2015). Families Coping: Effective Strategies for you and your child. Australian Council for Educational Research.

school or collect them. Additionally, keeping parents informed as to what is happening in the COPE-R program encourages ongoing family conversations.

Politeness

While some consider that children's acquisition of politeness is generally at the age of 5 or later (Pedlow, Sanson & Wales, 2004), children can be socialised into politeness earlier. Exposure to verbal forms such as "thank you", "please", and "I am sorry" is a feature of English and this appears in other cultures by the age of 3 in the form of greetings, polite expression, and language (Nakamura, 2006). So, it is both language and non-verbal acts that form the expression of kindness (Huebscher, Garufi & Prieto, 2019).

Empathic sharing

As children approach 2 years of age, they can understand themselves and they start displaying empathy and recognition of the feelings of others (Frydenberg et al., 2012; Pedlow et al., 2004). Empathy is described as individuals being able to understand and interpret the behaviour of others, to anticipate what someone else might do and feel, and then to respond to them (Allison et al., 2011; Baron-Cohen & Wheelwright, 2004).

While cognitive empathy comprises emotion recognition and perspective taking, emotional empathy includes the phenomenon of more adequate shared feelings with another person's situation, rather than with one's own. A more recent study revealed that emotional empathy development is complete in the pre-school years whereas cognitive empathy develops well into the school years (Schwenck et al., 2014).

For the young child the development of empathy for others is ongoing (Feshbach, 1982; Feshbach & Feshbach, 2009) and contingent on developing cognitive and emotional skills that enable the child to not only assume the perspective of another person but also to be able to feel and understand the emotional state of the person or the experience.

The recognition and naming of feelings also supports the development of empathy for others (Denham & Burton, 2003).

Development of the program

Working in collaboration with professionals in early childhood settings, the COPE-R program is part of a larger project undertaken to understand the social and emotional development of children of ages 4–8. From the inception of the early years coping project in 2010 we have set out to identify young children's articulation and understanding of coping constructs (Cornell et al., 2017; Deans, Frydenberg & Tsurutani, 2010). This was followed by a focus on developing children's coping skills through visual tools and classroom activities (Frydenberg & Deans, 2011). Previous projects have been conducted with parents and/or children enrolled at the University of Melbourne Early Learning Centre, with the Early Years Coping Cards being one of the project outcomes (Frydenberg & Deans, 2011). These cards have been commonly used to generate discussions with pre-schoolers about coping, and depict different situations a child may face using cartoon-like images. They have also been introduced to parents in the Families Coping: Preschool Parenting Program (Frydenberg, 2015). The cards and the parenting program have also been adapted for working with families with young children from culturally and linguistically diverse (CALD[3]) backgrounds (Deans et al., 2016) through a five-session community-based parenting program. The focus has been on helping parents to align their cultural practices with those of the local community, while at the same time endorsing the individual family's cultural practices, languages, and identity.

Program evaluation data shows that the use of culturally sensitive visual tools and tip sheets with core universal parenting principles, and the curation of a safe space to encourage sharing can affirm and expand parents' confidence in addressing the challenges faced during the everyday parenting journey and in sharing their experiences with others, thereby building community support beyond the program duration. The importance of effective parenting as a means for modelling and building social and emotional competence in young children and hence improving their wellbeing over time is the key takeaway message for parents.

Finally, these concepts and constructs have been incorporated into a COPE-R curriculum that has not only incorporated coping skills but also emphasised the development of empathy and prosocial behaviours. Several trials of the program have been reported (Cornell et al., 2017; Deans et al., 2017; Pang et al., 2018), each demonstrating the teaching of coping skills in the context of a social and emotional learning (SEL) program such as the COPE-R. The trials involved rating scales used by parents and teachers as well as assessing children's responses to challenging situations.

Taiwanese adaptation

The COPE-R program has also been adapted and trialled with a Chinese pre-school population in Taiwan. Like many Asian cultures, attitudes towards education in Taiwan have been heavily influenced by Chinese culture and the Confucian paradigm where the explicit teaching of emotion understanding, and regulation skills is still a new area for many educators. Taking into consideration the cultural context and the language, and while working closely with the early educators in Taiwan, a Chinese version of the COPE-R manual was created for trialling the program sequentially in three different pre-school communities, in which each stage was built upon the previous one. Wu, Alexander, Frydenberg and Deans' (2019) study shows that children undertaking the program demonstrated significant improvements in measures of emotional labelling, empathy, prosocial, coping style, and inhibitory control. The study also found that children who participated in the program demonstrated greater school readiness and fewer problem behaviours. Moreover, teachers also reported an increase in their understanding of emotions and ways to deal with challenging behaviours. Overall, it was found that even in culturally contrasted environments the implementation achieved beneficial outcomes for both the teacher and the children.

---

3 The term "culturally and linguistically diverse" (CALD) is commonly used in the research, practice, and policy discourse in Australia to refer to all of Australia's non-Indigenous ethnic groups other than the English-speaking Anglo-Saxon majority.

2 Implementation of COPE-R

Implementation of COPE-R

An overview of Part 2

i Program in brief

This section provides an overview of the implementation requirements of the program. It is highly recommended that you read this section before beginning the program.

ii Icon legends

This section provides a glossary of the activities used in the program and the icons used throughout the manual to identify each of the activities. Tips and ideas from experienced facilitators of the COPE-R program have been provided as well. You may like to review this section to decide which type of activity will best suit the needs of the children you are working with.

iii Important considerations for educators/facilitators

This section addresses the importance of establishing a safe environment, gaining children's attention, modelling, pedagogical practice, positive reinforcement, and what needs to be considered when working with children with trauma.

iv Program activities

This section includes all the activities required to implement the COPE-R program. It commences with developing the foundation skills for understanding emotions, followed by the five COPE-R topics:

- Topic 1: Caring for Others (C)
- Topic 2: Open Communication (O)
- Topic 3: Politeness (P)
- Topic 4: Empathic Sharing (E)
- Topic 5: Review (R)

v The teacher's experience and reflection

Over six years, an early childhood teacher has committed to implementing the COPE-R program with various groups of pre-school children. We have gathered her insights over the years and presented these throughout the text.

vi Supplementary materials for educators/teachers/facilitators

A list of reflective questions to guide processing and learnings from implementing the COPE-R program.

i Program in brief

This program is designed to assist you with the delivery of your current social emotional curriculum, in particular, in promoting empathy and prosocial behaviours in children.

In order to facilitate program delivery, the following points are highlighted:

- The **program is flexible**, and topics can be offered over multiple months or weeks, depending on the needs of your children.
- An important foundation skill for children to develop is **understanding emotions and empathy**; a selection of activities is provided to help build the foundational understanding of emotions for children. This understanding is the building block for each of the COPE-R topics. You can revisit these foundational skills with children such as *what feelings look like* and *noticing feelings in others*, **prior to the commencement** of each of the sessions.
- Individual **stand-alone activities have been created for each topic**; however, you are encouraged to reference previous concepts explored in the program to reinforce learning. You may provide parents/carers with information about each lesson (e.g., using a tip-sheet, discussions, etc.).
- A range of different styles of activities has been included. **Icons are provided throughout the manual** to identify the type of the activity (see Section ii for the icon legends).
- There are many ways to engage children in discussions about feelings, concerns, worries, or coping. The COPE-R program uses the **Early Years Coping Cards** as visual prompts, which are readily available online (via ACER online shop: https://shop.acer.edu.au). You can also use any of the following to facilitate the discussions:
    - Sets of situation and coping images are also available in Appendix 2 of this manual, which can be copied and laminated for personal use.
    - Toys such as "Worry Dolls" can be utilised.
    - Children's storybooks deal with a range of worrying situations, such as fear of animals, loss of a pet, a family move, or parental separation.
    - A collection of images depicting the worries and coping actions of children can be developed and/or compiled from discarded magazines or newspapers.
    - A unique set of images can be developed that suit the location and culture of an educational or a family setting.
- It is recommended that you deliver **a minimum of two activities** from the program in each week. Activities considered to be most important to achieving the objectives of the program are presented at the beginning of each topic. You will find "Optional Activities" presented at the end.
- At the **end of each week**, it is important to revisit the activities and revise the concepts taught to reinforce and consolidate learnings.
- Section vi provides a list of reflective questions to guide your processing and learnings from implementing the COPE-R program.
- This program contains many activities; however, you do not need to implement them all and you are welcome to **modify any activities** to suit the needs, interests, and abilities of the developmental stages of the children – i.e., you may want to make an activity more accessible to meet the needs of younger or older children.

ii Icon legends

Early Years Coping Cards[1]
These cards provide children with images of situations to help them explore their feelings, the feelings of others, and what they might do in the different situations presented. You can also use the images in Appendix 2 or alternatives.

Feelings Explorer
Feelings Explorer activities ask children to become a "Feelings Explorer", and engage in activities where they can think, explore, research, and discover social emotional skills.

Role-play
Role-play provides children with an opportunity to experience and practise the social emotional skills being explored in the program individually, in pairs, and in small groups. Role-play requires active involvement from the children and the educator/teacher/facilitator.

Art
Through drawing and drawing/telling children are given the opportunity to express their understandings of emotions and social behaviours.

Movement, Poetry, and Song
Through body movement, poetry, and song, children are encouraged to revisit the learning content in the program and celebrate their individual and group understandings.

Teaching Tips
Ideas from facilitators of COPE-R for integrating and implementing activities from different topic areas of the program into the daily curriculum.

---

[1] All images are from *The Early Years Coping Cards* (Frydenberg and Deans, 2011), published by the Australian Council for Educational Research (ACER Press).

Implementation of COPE-R

iii Important considerations for educators/facilitators

While educators/teachers/facilitators need to become familiar with the content of the lessons, important process components of the program will also assist children's learning and understanding. The following are some guidelines for consideration.

Create a safe and nurturing environment

- By creating a safe environment, children are able to learn more effectively. It is recommended the environment is accepting and warm, where positive relationships are encouraged. For example, you can simply start the day with circle time where all children sit down and look into each other's faces and greet each other with respect before you introduce the topic or concept for the day.

> *The introductions have been really important. It's amazing what children remember from every class introduction. Every time we have a COPE-R meeting there is excitement, and it's telling me the children are enjoying being in the sharing circle.*

- Recognise that children from culturally and linguistically diverse backgrounds are not homogenous and be aware of the potential influence of specific cultural factors on a child's behaviour and presentation. Asking for clarifications can help to avoid assumptions.
- Setting "ground rules" with the children can help them understand what acceptable behaviour is, e.g., listen quietly when someone is speaking; speak nicely to one another; be respectful to one another; look after one another.

> *It's almost as if you see something that is not visible, but it's actually there, such as a child ignoring another child, or a child walking in and sneakily going to do something. You sort of see those things straight away.*

Be a good "empathy" role model for children

> *I always say "good morning", and "should we say good morning to (X) this morning"? I am constantly subtly navigating. We keep the coping language in focus.*

- Young children imitate the behaviours of adults, so it is important that educators/teachers/facilitators model appropriate behaviours, in particular by focusing on exemplifying empathy and prosocial behaviours. Children are then more likely to also engage in these behaviours.
- It is recommended that educators/teachers/facilitators over-emphasise their use of feeling words when implementing COPE-R so it becomes commonplace for children to hear and use the language of coping.
- Although Topic 4 is dedicated to empathic sharing, **it is important that empathy is emphasised throughout every lesson**. Empathy is one of the most important social emotional skills to nurture within pre-schoolers. It is at the educator's discretion to highlight and incorporate empathy into the daily activities and curriculum.

> *When we engaged in the "threatened species day" we talked about empathy towards all the animals, so when an opportunity like that arises, we stop the group and use COPE-R even to tackle environmental issues, so COPE-R becomes integrated into everything we do.*

Encourage children to practise their skills during the day

- Developing empathy and prosocial behaviours can take time, especially when learning to take the perspective of another. Identify opportunities during the day to help children practise their skills, e.g., if there is conflict in the playground, ask each child how their behaviour has affected the other and how the other may be feeling.
- Use these opportunities to encourage independent problem solving rather than solving the problem for the child.

> *When I go outside, I always say, "Be kind to one another and every living thing", just reminding them often so that they go out to play feeling strong. Or I might speak to individual children who are often disruptive and say, "today, can you feel that some children are a little bit down, they're a little bit sad – could you keep an eye on them, and just be there for them". So I reverse the roles, and I empower the children who are having problems and I put them in a position where they can look after each other.*

Use positive reinforcement for appropriate behaviours

- Using specifically labelled praise (indicating what it is you are praising) is the best feedback for children as it specifically tells the child which behaviours are preferred and appropriate and allows them to learn the exact behaviour to be repeated. Labelled praise is more than just saying "good job", it is more specific; that is, you should identify the behaviour that is being approved, e.g., "Good job! I really liked how you helped your friend find the pencils".
- It is highly recommended that labelled praise be provided regularly when empathic and prosocial behaviours are observed.

> *Introduce the concepts and reinforce them every time, so children know what is coming. There are always ongoing discussions, either at an individual, small group, or big group level about respect, not just for each other but for the environment and the materials in the classroom. It is the circle time that generates most of the powerful understanding ... of anything that we do.*

Holding children's attention

- Keep discussions brief and focus on the activities.
- Use visual aids.
- Use techniques to gain children's attention, e.g., clapping in a pattern.
- Acknowledge children who are attending to the lesson.

> *Sometimes I put something beautiful in the middle of the group to indicate, for example, the arrival of spring – a beautiful crystal or a special book that a child has brought to share. Even acknowledging that on an individual level or in a small group level depending on what is going on (can guide children's attention).*

Working with children with trauma

- Young children may have experienced traumatic events such as illness or loss, or an environmental disaster such as bushfire, flood, or earthquake.
- Young children who have been through a traumatic experience may exhibit traumatic stress symptoms such as having difficulty regulating their behaviours and emotions. Some may be clingy and fearful of new situations, easily frightened, difficult to console, and/or aggressive and impulsive. They may also have difficulty sleeping, lose recently acquired developmental skills, and show regression in functioning and behaviour (McLean, 2016).
- Teachers need to be cognisant of changes in children's behaviour and sensitive when children are reluctant to participate in a particular activity.
- If there are concerns about a child's adaptations, the teachers will always be encouraged to discuss with senior staff, parents, or other allied professionals who can be a resource.
- In the context of classroom teaching, it would be appropriate for teachers to encourage children to use words and drawings to process and reflect on their emotions associated with lived experience.

iv Program activities

Overview of COPE-R activities

Foundation Skills: Understanding Emotions

Feelings Explorer: Finding Feelings
Feelings Explorer: Noticing Feelings in Others
Feelings Explorer: Pick a Feeling
Art: Feeling Faces
Feelings Explorer: Voice Chart
Role-play: What Feelings Look Like
Feelings Explorer: Quiet Spaces
Role-play: Guess the Emotion
Movement: Dance Our Feelings
Art: A Day of Feelings
Feelings Explorer: Coping with Feelings

Topic 1: Caring for Others (C)

Feelings Explorer: What is Caring?
Early Years Situation Card: Getting Hurt
Feelings Explorer: How Are You Feeling?
Feelings Explorer: Caring for the Environment
Feelings Explorer: Caring for Animals
Art: Animal Totems
Art: Caring Behaviours
Optional Activities
Art: Handmade Gifts for Each Other
Movement: Looking After Ourselves Too
Art: Caring Poems

Topic 2: Open Communication (O)

Early Years Situation Card: Wanting to Play with Others
Feelings Explorer: How a Good Listener Listens
Role-play: Supportive Statements
Movement: Types of Communication
Optional Activities
Art: Silence and Busyness

Topic 3: Politeness (P)

Early Years Situation Card: Bullied
Feelings Explorer: I'm Happy to Help
Feelings Explorer: Cultural Differences
Role-play: Polite Behaviours
Art: Friendly Cards
Movement: Bucket Filling

Topic 4: Empathic Sharing (E)

Early Years Situation Card: Choosing a Group to Play With
Feelings Explorer: How Can We Share
Role-play: Tricky Sharing Situations
Art: We Share a Life
Optional Activities
Movement: Creating a Sharing Poem/Song
Feelings Explorer: Understanding Others
Feelings Explorer: Helping Others Feel Better

Topic 5: Review (R)

Feelings Explorer: The Caring Tree
Feelings Explorer: Kind Acts
Role-play: Sharing from One Teapot
Art: Hunting and Gathering for Pleasant Feelings
Art: Sending Caring Messages Around the World
    Optional Activities
    Art: COPE-Resilience Game
    Movement: Creating a Mandala of Silence
    Mix and Match: Creating and Understanding Facial Expressions
    Rite of Passage: Training Resilience
    Suggestions from Educators

Foundation Skills: Understanding Emotions

> **Note**
>
> - Understanding emotions in oneself and in others provides a solid foundation for children to develop empathy and engage in prosocial behaviours. A selection of activities to help increase emotional intelligence has been provided for use prior to the commencement of the program and throughout. It is recommended that you use these activities as frequently as possible during the duration of the program.

Feelings Explorer: Finding Feelings

Aims

- To be able to identify different feelings as either pleasant or unpleasant.
- To be able to describe how pleasant and unpleasant feelings feel in our body.
- To be able to list a range of feeling words.

Materials

- Flipchart paper and pencil.

Preparation

- Prepare a flipchart paper with a vertical line down the middle, add headers to the two columns, e.g., soft versus hard or pleasant versus unpleasant, however you want to delineate the two different types of feelings.

Instructions

1. **Explain:** We all experience a range of feelings every day. Feelings are usually described in one word. Some feelings are pleasant to have, some are unpleasant. All feelings have a purpose, so they are not really good or bad. We sometimes experience them as soft versus hard feelings.
2. **Explain:** We are looking for feelings because they are part of our daily life and they make us who we are.
3. **Ask:**
    - What are you feeling right now?
    - Is that a pleasant or unpleasant feeling?
    - What feeling words do you know?
4. **Do:** Note the children's responses on the flipchart paper; encourage them to allocate their feeling suggestions to the appropriate column, e.g., pleasant/unpleasant, soft/hard, etc. Some examples are provided in the following box.

Pleasant/Soft Feelings		Unpleasant/Hard Feelings	
Happy	Surprised	Grumpy	Bored
Silly	Care	Cross	Angry
Relaxed	Trusting	Going bananas	Annoyed
Crazy	Friendly	Mad	Scared
Loving		Frustrated	

5. **Discuss:** Lead a discussion on how pleasant and unpleasant feelings feel in our body. Ensure children discuss how the basic feelings of happy, sad, angry, scared/frightened, and okay feel in the body.

Some examples are included below.

Example Responses

Pleasant/Soft Feelings:

- These make our bodies feel relaxed and happy.
- When you have these feelings your heart can go fast or slow.

Unpleasant/Hard Feelings:

- These make our bodies feel hard and shaky.
- When you have these feelings your heart can sometimes go angry fast or it can sometimes feel like your heart is a jellyfish.

Key Messages to Share

- It is important to ensure children can identify basic feelings of happy, sad, angry, scared/frightened, and okay.
- Ask the children to extend their responses by asking how they might feel in different situations, e.g., if they received a present, if they lost their favourite toy, etc.

Modification Suggestions for 3-year-old Group

* You might like to prepare picture card examples of facial expressions for children who have limited feeling words.
* You could choose to illustrate how feelings can be like colours, e.g., red is a very bright colour, so when we feel red, we may feel like doing something very quickly or loud, e.g., hitting, shouting, throwing things. Others may not want to be near someone when they feel red because they are afraid that they might get hurt.

* You can also discuss changing colour of emotions to something more calming, e.g., green and calm.
* Children can then be asked to think of a colour that represents an emotion and colour the words or pictures with the same colour.

Activity Example from a Teacher's Adaptation

Finding Feelings

Context: The teacher collected individual words by each child in the group, pointing out "feeling" words during the day when they were mentioned. Feelings words were then divided into Pleasant/Unpleasant. The teacher also helped children to find in between feelings, e.g., "You can be good nervous before the performance, and bad nervous if the principal calls you to the office when you know that you have made a friend feel sad."

Figure 2 Finding Feelings.

Feelings Explorer: Noticing Feelings in Others

Aims

- To be able to identify feelings in others.

I say, "could you please come and tell me if you notice that she is upset or crying". Giving children a special task helps them to rise up to the challenge.

Instructions

1. **Explain:** We are now going to talk about how our friends and family express their feelings.
2. **Ask:** What clues should we look for when trying to find out what another person is feeling?

Key Messages to Share

- It is important to watch and listen carefully to others to notice their feelings.
- You can tell how people are feeling by:

    o *Looking at their face.*
    o *Looking at their body.*
    o *Listening to their voice.*
    o *Looking at what's happening around them.*

3. **Discuss:** Lead a discussion on what different feelings look like in another person. Some examples are provided below — and you may like to expand and extend upon these ideas. It is recommended that you ask the children to show the feeling state on their face and through their body during this activity.

Feeling	Ask	Possible Responses
If a person is feeling **happy**:	What tone of voice might they use?	Light, easy, soft, or energised. Laughter.
	What might their body look like?	Smiling. Animated gestures. Standing up straight. Walking with a "bounce".
	What might have happened?	Having fun with friends. Playing with their favourite toy/game.

(Continued)

(Cont.)

If a person is feeling **angry**:	What tone of voice might they use?	Loud, bossy.
	What might their body look like?	Tight and tense body. Tight eyes and mouth. Holding hands in a fist.
	What might have happened?	Someone has snatched their favourite toy while they were playing with it.
If a person is feeling **sad**:	What tone of voice might they use?	Soft and low. Nervous voice.
	What might their body look like?	Slumped shoulders and hung head. Frown. Slow and heavy body.
	What might have happened?	Had to leave their parents. Fell over and got hurt.
If a person is feeling **excited**:	What tone of voice might they use?	Loud, energised. Laughter.
	What might their body look like?	Animated and moving around a lot. Eyes and mouth wide.
	What might have happened?	Receiving a present. About to go on a favourite outing.
If a person is feeling **scared** or **frightened**:	What tone of voice might they use?	Soft and low. Nervous voice. Whimper.
	What might their body look like?	Looking away/down. Tense. Arms around their chest. Shaking.
	What might have happened?	Had a bad dream. Nervous about first day of kinder. Heard a very loud noise.

Key Messages to Share

- When you know how another person is feeling, you can then decide how to show care for them so they feel you understand what they are experiencing.
- Some people might feel different feelings in response to the same situation. Discuss examples of this with the children, e.g., some people might be excited on their first day of kindergarten, while others may be nervous and scared. Some people might be sad when their toy is taken from them, but others may be angry.

   o Use puppet-play to illustrate how individuals might have different feelings in response to the same situation.

Feelings Explorer: Pick a Feeling

Aims

- To be able to identify a feeling recently experienced.
- To be able to describe the bodily sensations associated with a recent feeling.
- To be able to understand that others have a range of feelings.

Materials

- Cards with different feeling faces on them.
- A box containing the feeling cards to pass around.

Preparation

- Prepare a range of cards with different feeling faces on them (please use images with real faces, not illustrations), e.g., happy, sad, scared, surprised, okay, disgusted, angry, excited.

Instructions

1. **Explain:** I am going to pass around a box of feelings; look through the box and pick out a feeling that you have experienced recently. Tell the group your feeling, how you can tell that the person in the picture is experiencing this feeling, when you experienced it, and what it felt like in your body.
2. **Do:** Run the activity so that all children get a chance to select a feeling and talk about it.

Art: Feeling Faces

Aims

- To be able to identify feelings in others.

Materials

- Cards and pencils/crayons for the children to be able to draw feeling faces.
- A box to pass the feeling faces around in.

Instructions

1. **Do:** Have the children draw different feeling faces on cards, based on a feeling they have recently experienced. Encourage children to draw the situation in which they felt this feeling, e.g., a child draws feeling happy when playing with his/her dog. Once completed, these drawings are placed in a box.
2. **Explain:** We are now going to pass this box around, and when I ring the bell the person who has the box will pull out a picture and then we will discuss feelings that we see in the picture.
3. **Do:** Pass the box around the room, have each child select a card and identify the feeling on the card, and then have the child explain why they think it's that feeling, e.g., what about the face suggests that feeling.

Key Message to Share

- Some feelings can look similar, e.g., happy and excited, scared and sad. The children may not always guess the feeling correctly, so use this to discuss how some feelings have similar physical characteristics.

Modification Suggestions for 3-year-old Group

* You can use coping cards or prepare some Situation Cards for students who are unable to describe a situation or students who are unable to draw the situations.

Activity Example from a Teacher's Adaptation

Using sensory clay to create Clay Feelings
Context: A group of children used clay to create 2D clay faces depicting facial expressions that represent different feelings. As pictured here, the children's unique mark making produced a variety of expressions including, happy, sad, grumpy, funny, silly, concerned.

Figure 3 Clay Feelings.

Feelings Explorer: Voice Chart

Aims

- To be able connect feelings to classroom voice levels.

Materials

- A voice chart that has already been introduced to the class.

Preparation

- It is assumed that you have already introduced a voice chart into your classroom.

Instructions

1. **Explain:** We are now going to talk about soft and loud voices and how they express different feelings in different places.
2. **Do:** Lead a discussion around the possible feelings and atmosphere associated with each voice level in your classroom.

Voice Level	Possible Feelings/Atmosphere
0 – absolute silence, no one is talking.	Calm, thoughtful, reflective.
1 – whispering, only one person can hear you.	Calm, personal, focused on just one other.
2 – small group work, only the group can hear you.	Calm, focused, productive, everyone gets heard.
3 – normal conversation voice.	A bit more energised. The classroom can be loud and busy if everyone is using their normal conversation voice.
4 – presenting voice, everyone can hear you.	Loud voice, too loud for everyone to use, okay if just one person does.
5 – playground voice, never used in the classroom.	Loud, excited, can hurt your ears. Is painful to hear in a small space like a classroom.

Modification Suggestions for 3-year-old Group

* You can ask students to jump or move into different colour spots and adjust their voice level according to the colours.

Role-play: What Feelings Look Like

Aims

- To be able to identify the physical characteristics of different feelings.

Instructions

1. **Explain:** I am going to act out some different feelings, and I would like you to copy me. We can then guess what feelings they are!
2. **Do:** Create facial expressions and body gestures for different emotions and then ask the children what emotion you are all showing. Examples are below.

   - **Happy:** Stand up straight, smile, make your body loose and light, walk with a "bounce", laugh.
   - **Sad:** Slump your shoulders, hang your head, frown, make your body heavy, move slowly, sigh.
   - **Angry:** Squint your eyes, grit your teeth, tense your body, make your hands into fists.
   - **Scared:** Look away/down, tense your body, wrap your arms around your chest, shake a little, whimper.
   - **Disgusted:** Wrinkle your nose, tighten your stomach, say "eww".
   - **Surprised:** Open your mouth and eyes wide, move your head backwards and freeze your body, say "ohhh!".

Modification Suggestions for 3-year-old Group

* You may like to prepare a body template and point to various parts of the body associated with the emotions.
* You could also ask students to do simple movements in relation to big feelings (e.g., if you are happy, you clap your hands; if you are angry, cross your arms).
* You could also ask children to use animals as examples (how do you know if your pet is happy/sad/excited?) and get children to act out those actions.
* You may wish to ask children in your class to act out some movements and have other children to guess the emotions portrayed.

Activity Example from a Teacher's Adaptation

Creating a Classroom Poem about Feelings.

Context: A group of children reported seeing the full moon the night before and so the educator used "Moon" as the theme to create a poem about feelings.

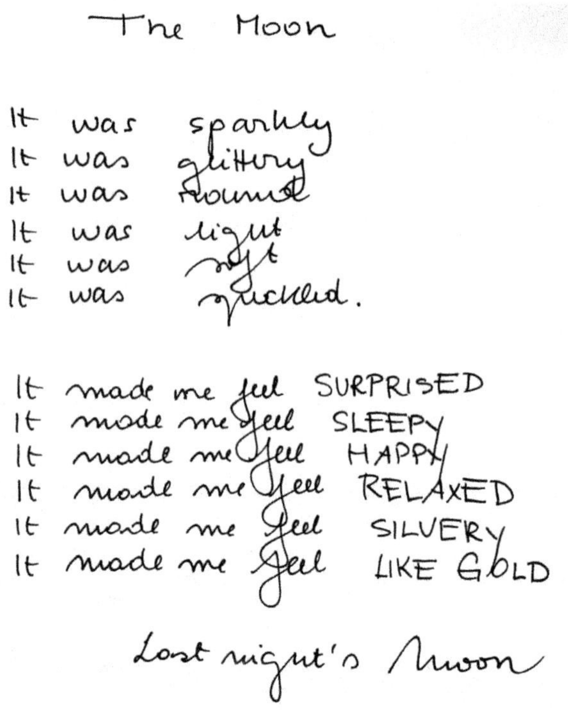

Implementation of COPE-R

The Moon

It was sparkly
It was glittery
It was round
It was light
It was soft
It was speckled.

It made me feel SURPRISED
It made me feel SLEEPY
It made me feel HAPPY
It made me feel RELAXED
It made me feel SILVERY
It made me feel LIKE GOLD

Last night's Moon

Figure 4 The Moon Poem.

Feelings Explorer: Quiet Spaces

Aims

- To be able to describe the importance of quiet time.
- To be aware of how to reduce strong emotions with quiet time.

We practise a silent moment of gazing which has been really good instead of just saying "sorry".

Materials

- A tent for only one child.
- A tub filled with water and pretty objects like rocks and flowers.
- A corner of the classroom with books and/or a selection of toys.
- Your own ideas.

Preparation

- Prepare two to three quiet spaces that best suit your classroom and your children.

Instructions

1. **Do:** Lead a discussion on how having quiet time on our own can help reduce strong feelings – for example, feeling sad about leaving mum or dad in the morning, or feeling angry that someone hurt your feelings during the day. Ask for examples of how quiet time has worked for the children in the past to reduce strong feelings.
2. **Do:** Lead a discussion on the rules for using the quiet spaces in your classroom – for example:

   - Only one child can use a space at a time.
   - If a child is using a quiet space, no other children can approach them.
   - You can use the quiet spaces at any time, even in the middle of an activity, and you will not get into trouble.
   - After a few minutes you might approach to check that you are okay.
   - Other rules as determined by your setting.

Role-play: Guess the Emotion

Aims

- To be able to display different feelings.
- To be able to identify feelings in others.

Instructions

1. **Do:** Ask the children to join up in pairs and role-play using body language and facial expressions for each other to guess the emotion.
2. **Do:** When the other child has had a chance to guess, have the children swap roles so that they both get a chance to display a feeling and also guess a feeling.
3. **Discuss:** Lead a discussion on how the children were able to identify the feeling the other person was displaying. Note, some feelings can look similar, e.g., happy and excited, scared and sad. Also encourage the children to discuss what feelings have similar physical characteristics.

Movement: Dance Our Feelings

Aims

- To revise what feelings look like.

Instructions

1. **Do:** Play an upbeat (happy) song and ask the children to dance to the song and display appropriate emotions with their body and face.
2. **Ask:**
   - How did this music make you feel?
   - How did you show your emotions with your body and your face?
3. **Do:** Repeat steps 1 and 2, with different types of songs, e.g., a slow tempo (sad) song, a loud (angry) song, an upbeat (exciting) song, etc.

Activity Example from a Teacher's Adaptation

Composing Music Using Drawings

Context: Children were asked to compose a piece of music using drawings and to articulate the feelings associated with the creative piece.

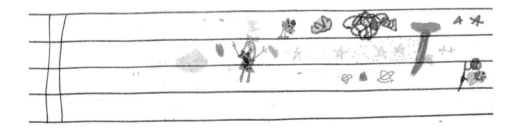

Figure 5 Composing music.

This illustrated piece in Figure 5 by a 4-year-old child shows "soft music that gets opened with the red love heart key". "It should be played by tinkling bells, it sounds happy and magical."

Art: A Day of Feelings

Aims

- To be able to draw and describe a day of feelings.
- Understand how different events or situations might impact our feelings.
- Understand how our feelings are always changing.

Materials

- Paper and pencils/crayons for the children to be able to draw a day of feelings.

Instructions

1. **Do:** Ask the children to draw a picture of a day that made them feel a strong emotion or different emotions over the day, e.g., happy, sad, scared, etc. Have the children sit some distance apart so that they have the space to draw and not copy each other.
2. **Do:** Ask the children to sit in a circle and describe their day and picture one by one. Ask them to identify what about the picture shows the feeling(s) associated with the day.

Modification Suggestions for 3-year-old Group

* You may like to prepare a feeling thermometer as a visual to illustrate changes in feelings.

Figure 6 Children's version of a feeling thermometer.

Feelings Explorer: Coping with Feelings

Aims

- Develop positive coping behaviours for dealing with difficult feelings.

When dealing with fear I said, "You know, if you keep this stone in your pocket all the time, and if you touch it, and you hold it, and you warm it, just at the time when your mum is about to leave, it will give you special powers. The child asked, "can you write the word brave on it", so we used a golden pen to write "brave" on his stone that is now sitting in his pocket all the time. And that was one really simple thing that helped him to cope.

Materials

- Flipchart and pencil.

Instructions

1. **Explain:** We have been learning a lot about the different feelings we all experience. Some are nice feelings, and some are not so nice! Let's talk about how we can cope with unpleasant feelings.
2. **Ask:** How can we cope when we feel:
    - Sad
    - Angry
    - Frustrated
    - Scared
    - Disappointed
    - Jealous
    - Hurt?
3. **Discuss:** Lead a discussion on the ways that the children have coped with these feelings, or what they think they might do to cope, e.g., tell a parent/teacher/friend, take deep breaths to calm down, do something fun that makes me happy, etc.
4. **Do:** Draw a chart, mind-map, or list of the children's responses.

Note

- You might like to display the chart created for children to see in the classroom, to use as a reminder when children experience negative emotions and to reinforce positive coping behaviours.

Implementation of COPE-R

Modification Suggestions for 3-year-old Group

* You may like to prepare a jar of small balloons and get children to take out one balloon each and squeeze it. Children can practise breathing while squeezing as a calming strategy. You may want to check if any children could be intimidated by popping balloons.
* You could also encourage children to squeeze other soft objects while breathing, such as sand.
* You could also choose to demonstrate in the following way: all of us can cope with unpleasant feelings; we can release the unpleasant feelings, just like how we squeeze and release the air out of the balloon or with sand. When we feel calm, we can then help others who are in need. You could prompt the children to brainstorm on what other things they could do to release unpleasant feelings.

Topic 1: Caring for Others (C)

> When we are nice and calm with our friends
> (Quote from a group of pre-school children)

Feelings Explorer: What Is Caring?

Aims

- To be able to describe different caring actions.

Instructions

1. **Explain:** We are now going to talk about what it means to care for ourselves and others.
2. **Do:** Use butcher paper to record children's responses on a mind-map,[2] separated into sections on caring for yourself, other people, animals, the environment, and the world.
3. **Ask:**

    - What is caring?
    - How do we care for other people?
    - How do we care for other living things, e.g., our environment, animals?
    - What kind of caring actions can we do?

        ■ Caring actions towards other people

        ● Say:

            ○ Say something nice, e.g., a compliment.
            ○ Stick up for others – speak up when someone is hurting someone else's feelings.

        ● Do:

            ○ Give someone a hug.
            ○ Offer to help, e.g., around the house or at school.

Listen to others.

        ■ Caring actions towards other living things

        ● Say:

            ○ Tell people about how to care for their environment, e.g., how to recycle.
            ○ Ask people to pick up their rubbish.
            ○ Stick up for animals – speak up when someone is being unkind to an animal.

---

[2] Mind-maps are diagrams for representing tasks, words, concepts, or items linked to and arranged around a central concept that allow us to build connections between different elements.

- Do:
    - Pat animals safely and gently.
    - Put rubbish in the correct bin.

- Describe a time when you were caring towards another person or living thing.

Key Messages to Share

- We can show our caring for others or living things in many ways. We might each prefer to show our caring in our own way, but all caring actions are valued.
- Caring actions may be in the form of either "Say" or "Do". Children may show they care for others by saying something or doing something.
- Not only can someone else feel good when we care for them, but we can also feel good about ourselves.

Implementation of COPE-R

Early Years Situation Card: Getting Hurt

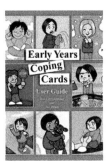

Aims

- To be able to identify when someone is upset.
- To be able to describe ways to care for someone who is upset.

Materials

- Early Years Situation Card "Getting Hurt".
- Alternatives: Images from Appendix 2 or other substitutes.

Instructions

1. **Explain:** There are many ways we can care for others; caring for others is especially important when others are upset.
2. **Ask:** How do we know if someone is upset?
3. **Do:** Show the children the situation card "Getting Hurt".
4. **Ask:**

    - What is happening in this picture?
    - What do you think the boy is feeling?
    - How would you feel?
    - Has this situation ever happened to you?
    - What could you do to care for this boy?

Figure 7 Getting Hurt Situation Card.

Implementation of COPE-R

> **Key Messages to Share**
>
> - The boy has fallen over and hurt his knee; he might feel sad, hurt, upset, worried, etc.
> - You could care for him by sitting with him, getting help from an adult, giving him a hug, telling him he will be okay.
> - It's important to look out for your friends, particularly when they look upset, and to show them that you care.

> **Note**
>
> - You might like to role-play this situation with the children and ask for volunteers to play along.

Activity Example from a Teacher's Adaptation

Discussions Around Getting Hurt

Context: A group of children were prompted to have a discussion around getting hurt using the Early Years Coping Card and were asked to provide examples of coping strategies.

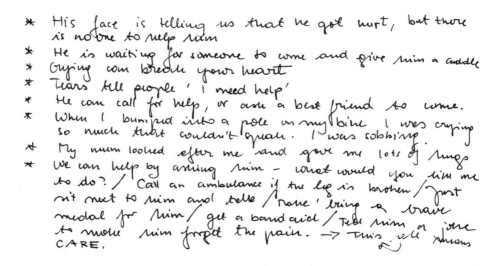

Figure 8 Children's discussion on the "Getting Hurt" Situation card.

Implementation of COPE-R

Feelings Explorer: How Are You Feeling?

Aims

- To be able to identify current feelings.
- To be able to care for another based on their feelings.

Materials

- A poster that lists a range of feelings common to the children's age group, e.g., happy, sad, angry, okay, scared, excited, nervous, shy.
- Photos of each child in the classroom.

Preparation

- Prepare the feelings poster and photos so that the children can readily move their photos next to the relevant feeling. Consider laminating the poster and photos.

Instructions

1. **Explain:** Discuss each feeling listed and explain that they will be asked to post their photo next to the feeling they are feeling the most at different times during the week.
2. **Do:** Ask the children to post their photo next to a feeling at different times of the day, e.g., first thing in the morning and then again after lunch.
3. **Do:** Lead a discussion after the children have posted their photos. Notice if some feelings changed from the morning to the afternoon. Notice both pleasant and unpleasant feelings among the group. If someone is feeling sad, scared, nervous, etc., discuss ways to provide support to help them feel more positive that day.

> **Key Messages to Share**
>
> - Feelings change throughout the day; they rarely stay the same.
> - We can notice feelings in others and help cheer them up if they are feeling down.
> - If we know how others are feeling, we can better help and support them.
> - It can feel good to share our feelings and have others support us, if necessary.

Feelings Explorer: Caring for the Environment

Aims

- Encourage respect and caring actions towards the environment.
- Increase awareness of how our actions can impact the environment.
- Highlight the importance and significance of our natural environment.
- Develop empathy towards the environment.
- Foster advocacy towards threatened aspects of the environment.

*We are seeing for the first time [in my 35-year teaching career] parents reporting that children have nightmares because of ecological disasters and climate change because they saw the Amazon burning. They saw fires. For **empathy**, we often focus on the individuals and groups. I think the empathy towards **nature** needs to be stepped up; we need to develop a sense of activism, e.g., "I can do it", **"I can help in a small way but in a meaningful way"**. You can talk about the voice of the sea, and the voice of the forest.*

Preparation

- Organise field trip to an area of the natural environment significant to your local community.
- Prepare teaching content on a threatened aspect of your local environment, e.g., local wildlife, endangered species, heritage building, trees/plant species.

Instructions

1. **Do:** Visit and explore an area of the natural environment significant to your local community.
2. **Ask:** What kinds of caring actions would benefit the site you are visiting.
3. **Discuss:** Lead a discussion on what current environmental threats there are to the site, and what kinds of things are being done to protect and care for it.
4. **Do:** Assess whether there is a need for action by a body such as the local council or government to help care for or protect an aspect of the environment. If so, you may like to assist the children in writing a letter sharing their views and things they have learnt on the issue, in order to advocate for action.

Note

- This activity may be modified to suit what is relevant and practical for your setting. It may occur over a prolonged period rather than in one sitting.

Modification Suggestions for 3-year-old group

* You may take some photos of the place visited and display the photos to facilitate discussion with the students.
* You may help students to do some artwork focusing on the beauty of the place visited as an alternative to the letter. Then make a picture collage out of their art pieces.

Feelings Explorer: Caring for Animals

Aims

- Encourage respect and caring actions towards animals.
- Increase awareness of how our actions can impact animals.
- Help children expand their understanding of caring and empathy beyond other people to include animals.
- Enhance caring and empathy towards animals by helping children identify with animals.

Materials

- Storybooks that feature animals and depict themes of kindness, strength and empathy.
- Examples:
  - *The Heart of a Whale* by Anna Pignataro.
  - *Two Hearted Numbat* by Ambelin Kwaymullina and Ezekiel Kwaymullina.
  - *Tomorrow I'll Be Kind* by Jessica Hische.

Instructions

1. **Read:** During group time, read the story of choice. Use animated storytelling to emphasise the illustrations of the character's journey.
2. **Ask:** You can use the following questions for engaging children in the storytelling:

   - What do you think is happening here? What do we think about that?
   - How do you think the whale/numbat/rabbit is feeling?
   - What do you think about the whale/numbat/rabbit's choice? What else could they do? Why do you think it that is important?
   - What kind of personalities do we have that are not described in the book?
   - What do they tell about our feelings, moods, and actions?

3. **Discuss:** Use the story to spark further discussion on other animals and the different personalities they display or feelings they might experience.

Art: Animal Totems

Aims

- For children to be able to identify and communicate their understanding of their own feelings and imagine animals who might share the same according to their behaviour.

Materials

- Coloured pencils/crayons.
- Small squares of brown and white paper to draw out an animal that represents you.

Preparation

- Have an example prepared of your own animal totem to help children understand the task. Use pencils and small squares of paper to create an animal that represents you and explain how the animal's characteristics are similar to yours.

Instructions

1. **Explain:** Different kinds of animals are unique in the ways that they think, feel, and behave – just like people. We can imagine how our own personalities might match a particular animal.
2. **Ask:**
   - What is the totem animal? Do we all have one? What kind of animal agrees with you?
   - Why do some specific animals resonate with us?
   - What does this tell us about our feelings moods and actions?
3. **Do:** Ask children to draw their spirit animal using materials listed above.
4. **Discuss:**
   - How many different totems do we have in our classroom?
   - What are the relationships between the totems?
   - What kind of thread can the children identify among their totems?
   - Find and group the animal totems children have chosen according to shared characteristics.

Modification Suggestions for 3-year-old Group

* You could also prepare some animal pictures for students who are unable to draw and ask them to decorate their totem.

Art: Caring Behaviours

Aims

- To be able to describe and draw a range of caring behaviours.

Materials

- Paper.
- Coloured pencils/crayons.

Instructions

1. **Explain:** There are many ways we can show how we care for others. I want you to think about a time when you have been kind or cared for another, e.g., given someone a hug when they were upset, shared your toy, cuddled your pet, etc.

Focus on broadening children's knowledge about the types of caring we can engage in and use themes explored in the earlier activities. Some options include:

- Caring for friends.
- Caring for family.
- Caring for the environment.
- Caring for animals.

Figure 9 Caring for all living creatures.

Implementation of COPE-R

2. **Ask:** Who has an example they can share with the class?
3. **Do:** Have the children each draw a picture of a situation where they cared for another.
4. **Do:** After the children have completed their drawings, ask them to sit in a circle and describe their picture one by one. Also have them answer the following question: "How did the other person/animal/living thing feel after you cared for them?"

Activity Example from a Teacher's Adaptation

Caring Behaviours

Context: Teacher asked children to think of a time when they have been kind or cared for something or someone and express it in writing and drawing.

Figure 10 Caring for family.

Implementation of COPE-R

Activity Example from a Teacher's Adaptation

Caring for the World

Context: Children discussed ways to care for our world.

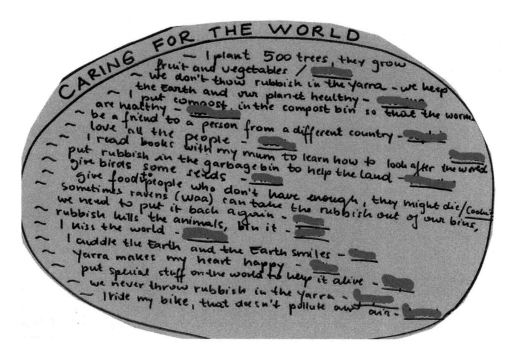

Figure 11 Caring for the world.

Note

- You may want to share some examples to assist children who may be having difficulties thinking of appropriate situations.
- If children say they haven't engaged in any caring behaviours, encourage them to think about what caring acts they could do.

Key Message to Share

- Aim to extend the children's understanding of caring beyond their immediate friends and family to understanding that we can also care for our wider community and even the world.

Modification Suggestions for 3-year-old Group

* Option: You could also play a "Happy Chair" game. Children will take turns to sit on the chair and have others say nice things about them. Educator can facilitate a discussion on kind words or simple phrases and write down those model scripts, e.g., "You are very good at drawing!", or "It makes me happy to see you saying kind words to your friends".) on cards. Children can pick up the cards and say them to their friends. Drawings and symbols can be used too.

Optional Activity

Art: Handmade Gifts for Each Other

Aims

- To be able to display and receive a caring behaviour within the classroom.

Instructions

1. **Do:** Give the children a task to make a gift or card for a friend or family member. You could also make a gift or card for someone you don't know very well in your class. Allow one day to complete this task.
2. **Do:** After the task has been completed, lead a discussion about what it felt like to give and receive the handmade or found gifts.
3. **Do:** Extend on the above task by asking the children to draw out a name from a box. Allow approximately one day for the children to complete this task.
4. **Do:** After the task has been completed, again discuss what it felt like to give and receive the handmade or found gifts.

Implementation of COPE-R

Optional Activity

Movement: Looking After Ourselves Too

Aims

- To recognise that we can get overwhelmed by other people's emotions.
- To be able to apply breathing techniques to calm ourselves down.

Instructions

1. **Ask:** How might we feel if we are caring for someone who is not happy?

> **Key Message to Share**
> - Explain that, when we are caring towards someone else, sometimes we can become overwhelmed by our own feelings, e.g., crying, withdrawing, running away, and may not be able to think about how to care for the other person.

2. **Ask:** What can we do if we are feeling very upset/worried/angry when another person is not happy?
3. **Explain:** We are now going to practise taking slow deep tummy breaths and counting to 10 to help us learn to calm down.
4. **Do:** Together with the children, practise taking deep tummy breaths, followed by slowly counting to and then back from 10.
5. **Ask:** Ask the children how they now feel, e.g., a little bit more relaxed/calmer?
6. **Explain**: We can also remind each other to use these strategies when we notice someone else is not feeling calm.

> **Facilitator Note**
> - See Appendix 1 for more advanced mindfulness and relaxation techniques. These will need to be adapted to suit the age of the children.

Optional Activity

Art: Caring Poems

Aims

- To be able to display and receive a caring behaviour in the form of a poem.

Instructions

1. **Do:** Ask the children to write a poem for someone in the classroom or a family member. Assist younger children to document their poems.
2. **Do:** Request the children to give their poems to the intended receiver today or tonight.
3. **Do:** Ask for some volunteers to share their poem with the class.

Note

- Follow up on this activity the next day and discuss how children felt after receiving their poems.

Topic 2: Open Communication (O)

When you listen with your whole body you understand every message, even the ones that are silent

(Quote from a group of pre-school children)

Early Years Situation Card: Wanting to Play with Others

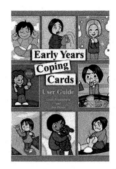

Aims

- To be able to communicate something important.

Materials

- Early Years Situation Card "Wanting to Play with Others".
- Alternatives: Images from Appendix 2 or other substitutes.

Instructions

1. **Explain:** Sometimes we feel like we want to say something that is important to us, but we find it difficult to say it.
2. **Ask:** What are some examples of things that are important but difficult to say?

> **Key Message to Share**
> - Allow for individual responses from the children. Some examples might be, needing to go to the toilet, wanting to join in a game, letting someone know they have hurt your feelings, sharing an opinion, saying no to something.

3. **Do:** Show the children the Situation Card "Wanting to Play with Others".
4. **Ask:**

- What is happening in this picture?
- What do you think the girl in the green top is feeling?
- How would you feel?
- Has this situation ever happened to you?
- What could the girl in the green top say?

Implementation of COPE-R

Figure 12 "Wanting to Play with Others" Situation Card.

Key Messages to Share

- The girl could respond accurately about her feelings and say: "That looks like fun, could I play too".
- The girl could respond not according to her feelings, or defensively, and say: "I don't want to play with you guys, what you're doing looks dumb".
- It's important to communicate accurately about our feelings so that people know and understand what we want them to know – people are not mind readers!

Feelings Explorer: How a Good Listener Listens

Aims

- To be able to describe the difference between listening and hearing.
- To be able to identify good listening skills.

Materials

- Flipchart/whiteboard.

Instructions

1. **Ask:** What do you think the difference between hearing and listening is?

> **Key Message to Share**
> - We hear with our ears, but we listen with our ears, brains, and even our hearts. When you listen you really pay attention to what the other person is saying, and you think about what they are feeling. Listening to others helps us understand and imagine how they are thinking or feeling in their situation

2. **Explain:** Most of us have great hearing, but we are not always good listeners. Let's see if you can identify a very soft sound or a whisper and then talk about what we need to do to be a good listener.
3. **Ask:**
    - What are some things a good listener does to show they are listening?
    - Think about what someone does with their face and body to show they are listening to you.
    - It might also help to remember a time when someone really listened to you.

4. **Do:** Ask a child to volunteer to draw a human body. Individual children can then be invited to add to the drawing by identifying functions of the specific parts of the body that are involved in hearing and listening, e.g., brain, ears, eyes, heart, posture, facial expressions (see Figure 13 below for example).

Implementation of COPE-R

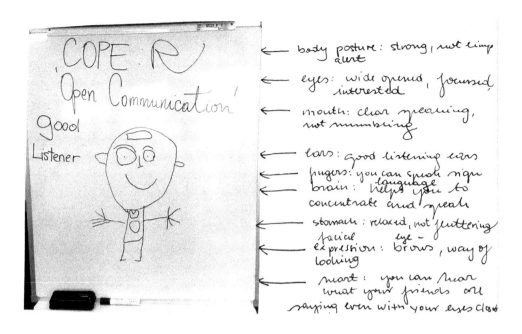

Figure 13 Listening with the whole body.

Figure 14 A good listener.

Role-play: Supportive Statements

Aims

- To be able to explain the importance of supportive statements.
- To be able to identify appropriate expressions of concern for others.

Materials

- Two puppets.
- A stage for the puppet role-play.

Instructions

1. **Explain:** When someone tells you something good, it can be easy to know what to say, e.g., "congratulations", "well done", "I'm happy for you". It can be harder to know what to say when someone tells you something bad. Sometimes you might want to say something encouraging like, "don't worry, I bet you'll do better next time", while at other times you might just say something that shows you are aware of their feelings like, "I'm sorry your dog ran away, you must feel really sad about that".
2. **Ask:**

    - Have you ever felt like you didn't know what to say to someone?
    - What did you do?

3. **Explain:** Explain that you will now role-play with puppets two possible responses to a situation and the children have to vote on the best response at the end. Select two or more role-play scenarios most appropriate to your class or create your own!
4. **Do:** At the end of each puppet show have the children vote on the best response and discuss why they chose it.

Scenario A: One of the puppets wants to join a soccer team but his mum has said no as he is already doing enough activities. The puppet is feeling sad and disappointed he can't join the team. The other puppet is asking what the matter is and responding as below.

Response 1: *My other friend Sam is on that soccer team!*	**Response 2:** *I'm sorry you can't join the team.*

Scenario B: One of the puppets is sad because their pet bunny is sick and has to stay at the vet's to get better. The other puppet is asking what the matter is and responding as below.

Response 1: *I'm really sorry to hear about your bunny. Is there anything I can do to help?*	**Response 2:** *Don't worry about it, let's play chasey.*

(Continued)

(Cont.)

Scenario C: One of the puppets is upset because they weren't invited to Sally's birthday party. The other puppet is asking what the matter is and responding as below.

Response 1: *Don't worry about it, it'll be your birthday soon and you can invite everyone except Sally.*

Response 2: *Try not to let it worry you too much, not everyone was invited, just a few of Sally's friends.*

Scenario D: One of the puppets is sad because they lost their favourite teddy bear at the weekend. The other puppet is asking what the matter is and responding as below.

Response 1: *I'm sorry you lost your favourite teddy. You must feel really sad about that.*

Response 2: *Do you want me to buy you a new teddy?*

Movement: Types of Communication

Aims

- To be able to identify and display various verbal and non-verbal communication messages.

Materials

- Prepared drawing of a child.
- Markers.

Instructions

1. **Explain:** Communication means passing on thoughts, feelings, or information. We communicate in lots of different ways.
2. **Do:** Show how we can use our head and face to communicate:

    - Use your head to communicate "yes".
    - Use your head to communicate "no".
    - Use your face to communicate you are "happy".
    - Use your face to communicate you are "sad".
    - Use your face to communicate you are "surprised".
    - Use your face to communicate you are "scared".

3. **Do:** Show how we can use our hands and arms to communicate:

    - Use your hands to say, "three".
    - Use your hands to say, "shhhh".
    - Use your hands to say, "I can't hear you".
    - Use your hands and arms to say, "goodbye".
    - Use your hands and arms to say, "go away".
    - Use your hands and arms to say, "I don't know".

4. **Do:** Have the children in a circle. Ask them to communicate in the ways suggested above. When the children respond accurately, use labelled praise as positive reinforcement and also model the non-verbal communication offered by the children. Encourage the children to exaggerate what you ask them to do and to have fun with it.
5. **Explain:** We can use our entire body to communicate.

    - Use your whole body to say, "I'm confident".
    - Use our whole body to say, "I'm angry".
    - Use your whole body to say, "I'm shy".
    - Use your hands to say, "three".

6. **Explain:** Talking is another way we communicate. Sometimes we only need one word or phrase to communicate, such as, "yes", "no", "sorry", "thanks", "go away", "come here", "don't", "please". Sometimes we use more than one word.

Optional Activity

Art: Silence and Busyness

Aims

- To reflect on the value of silence through discussion and art.

Materials

- Paper and pencils/crayons for the children to draw with.

Materials

- Draw a vertical line down the middle of each piece of paper.

Instructions

1. **Do:** Discuss the value of silence. Where we can find silence and what we can learn from silence. Discuss what we can communicate via silence and what we can understand from another person's silence.
2. **Explain:** Explain to the children that you want them to draw silence on one side of their piece of paper and busyness/loudness on the other side of the line.
3. **Do:** Ask the children to sit in a circle and describe their picture one by one.

> **Key Messages to Share**
>
> - "Busyness is moving".
> - "Stillness is our thinking position".

Implementation of COPE-R

Topic 3: Politeness (P)

> We say "thank you" and "yes please". It means looking after people.. listening to each other, everybody.
>
> (Quote from a group of pre-school children)

Early Years Situation Card: Bullied

Aims

- To learn how to be friendly/polite to others.
- To understand the impact of unfriendly/impolite behaviours on others.

Materials

- Early Years Situation Card "Bullied".
- Alternatives: Images from Appendix 2 or other substitutes.

Instructions

1. **Explain:** Being unfriendly and impolite to others can make them feel unhappy and they actually may not even want to be our friend.
2. **Do:** Show the children the Situation Card "Bullied".

Figure 15 Bullied Situation Card.

3. **Ask**:

- What is happening in this picture?
- What are some unfriendly/impolite behaviours shown in this picture?
- What do you think each boy is feeling? How would you feel?

- Has this situation ever happened to you? What did you do?
- What would be some friendly/polite behaviours for this situation?

Key Messages to Share

- The taller boy is teasing the shorter boy because he cannot reach the toy. The taller boy is not listening to the shorter boy
- The taller boy looks happy but unfriendly. The shorter boy could be feeling frustrated, angry, upset, and even scared.
- Teasing others is unfriendly/impolite behaviour and can make others unhappy.
- The taller boy could be polite/friendly by sharing the toy with the shorter boy and offering to play with him.

Feelings Explorer: I'm Happy to Help

Aims

- To introduce the concept of being happy to help others.
- To learn friendly and polite words and to practise using them in everyday situations.

You can see the child being impolite, you can see who is expressing empathy towards each; you've developed this sixth sense of what's going on around the class in the classroom through a COPE-R lens all the time and you see what you didn't see before.

Preparation

- It is recommended that this activity be implemented during times when the children are all together and can practise being friendly and polite in an everyday situation, e.g., lunch time, pack up time, during a group activity.

Instructions

1. **Explain:** There are some useful words we can use to be friendly and polite. For example, if someone needs assistance, we can say "I'm happy to help you".
2. **Ask:** What are some other friendly and polite words/expressions?

> **Key Messages to Share**
>
> - Examples of friendly/polite expressions: "I am happy to help"; "thank you", "please", "excuse me", "may I?", "can I?", "could I?", "I am sorry", "well done", "I appreciate this/you", "these fruit and flowers are nice", "oh that is lovely/beautiful", "my pleasure", "I love you", "I don't like this/want to do this, but thank you for thinking of me".
> - Using friendly and polite expressions helps to create a friendly and happy environment and helps to build friendships.

3. **Do:** During a group activity, e.g., lunch time, etc., role model friendly/polite expressions/behaviours, and encourage the children to do the same with each other. Continue to reinforce these behaviours throughout the day with the children.

> **Note**
>
> - You may like to write the examples generated on paper and display them in the room as reminders for children.

Feelings Explorer: Cultural Differences

Aims

- To learn how some different cultures/families show friendliness and politeness.
- To learn to be respectful of different cultural/family traditions and customs.

Materials

- Flipchart paper and markers.

Instructions

1. **Explain:** Being polite and friendly means we also respect each other's differences. Our world is made of up of many people from different countries and cultures, which makes it a very interesting place to be! Some cultures and families may express politeness and gratitude in different ways.
2. **Ask:** What are some different cultures? What do you do in your home to show politeness? What are some examples of your specific family/cultural traditions?
3. **Do:** On flipchart paper, write examples generated by the children (and/or use the examples below) to illustrate the difference between some Western and Non-Western cultures. Discuss the importance of respecting different traditions and beliefs from your own as a way of being polite.

Examples of Polite/Friendly Behaviours

Some Western Cultures	Some Non-Western Cultures
Looking at others when talking and/or listening.	Some Asian cultures – *not* looking directly at an elder when talking and/or listening.
Eating all of the food on your plate.	Some Asian cultures – leaving some food on the plate shows respect for the food provided.
When entering someone's house, shoes usually remain on the feet.	Some Asian cultures – shoes are removed before entering a house.
Waving, shaking hands, hugging, and/or kissing are used to greet others.	Some Asian cultures – nodding with a smile or bowing is a common greeting.
Talking to your brothers and sisters.	Some Indian cultures – *not* polite to talk to your brother if you are female and vice versa.

(*Continued*)

(Cont.)

Individuals outside of the family are generally termed as "friends". Terms "brother"/"sister" are usually used exclusively for brothers and sisters.	Some Asian cultures – individuals outside of their family are commonly termed as "brother" or "sister" as a sign of belonging.
It is polite to talk to all family members.	Some Indigenous Australian cultures – it is polite to ask another person to talk to "the mob" rather than an individual person.

Note

- You may like to role-play these examples with the children.
- You may want to include other examples that are relevant to the cultural background of the children in your room.

Modification Suggestions for 3-year-old Group

* You may prepare some visuals or videos to illustrate cultural differences, e.g., eating etiquettes, ceremonies, clothing, festivals, tea drinking, food.

Role-Play: Polite Behaviours

Aims

- To practise polite and friendly behaviours using different scenarios.

Preparation

- It is recommended this activity be implemented once children have a good understanding of friendly and polite behaviours.
- Decide whether you would like the children to do the role-plays in pairs, in a small group, or as a whole class exercise.

Instructions

1. **Ask:** Think about what it means to be friendly and polite. What are some examples of friendly and polite behaviours?
2. **Explain:** We are now going to practise being friendly and polite to one another by acting out some different scenarios (examples are provided below).
3. **Do:** If not doing a whole class role-play, instruct children to form pairs or small groups, and visit each pair/group with a scenario to role play.

Examples of Scenarios

- You want to get your friend's attention; how would you do this in a polite way? (e.g., approach your friend, smile, say hello).
- A child is tapping the table loudly with a pencil. How can you deal with this in a friendly way? (e.g., in a normal voice, ask the child to stop; inform the educator).
- You accidentally bump into another child and they are hurt. What could you do? (e.g., say sorry, take him/her to the educator).
- You see a child alone at lunch time and they look unhappy. How can you deal with this in a friendly way? (e.g., approach the child, smile, ask him/her if s/he would like to join you, etc.).
- A child throws an object at you in the playground. What could you do? (e.g., in a normal voice, tell him/her to stop; if s/he doesn't stop, move away from the child and inform the educator).
- Your best friend is playing with another child and s/he does not want to play with you. What could you do? (e.g., tell him/her you feel sad; find another child to play with).
- A child is teasing/being mean to another child. What could you do? (e.g., ask the child to stop teasing and suggest a game to play).
- You are playing a game with two of your friends and they start fighting. How could you manage this situation? (e.g., suggest they stop fighting and instead have fun together; suggest a different game; inform the educator).

Implementation of COPE-R

4. **Do:** If the children are in pairs or small groups, observe their role-plays and provide suggestions and encouragement as necessary. Following the role-play, ask or choose some children to act out their scenario for the rest of the class and ask them to identify the friendly and polite behaviours.

Note

- To assist the children with the role-plays, reminders about how to be polite and friendly may be displayed on a poster in the room.
- You may like to do a role-play with the whole class first, followed by paired or group role-plays.

Art: Friendly Cards

Aims

- To create a collection of friendly cards as reminders of how to be friendly and polite with others.
- To learn to be friendly and polite during a paired activity.

Materials

- Cardboard and markers for children to use to create their own cards.

Preparation

- Organise children into pairs.

Instructions

1. **Explain:** We are going to create some "friendly" cards to remind us about friendly/polite behaviours. I want each pair to create one or two cards by working together on each card. One of you might like to draw a picture and the other may like to colour it in. Remember to use your friendly/polite behaviours while you are working together.
2. **Ask:** Once the cards have been completed, ask each pair to present their cards to the rest of the group and discuss how they were friendly/polite to one another during the activity

> **Key Messages to Share**
>
> - By being friendly/polite we are respecting others and creating a warm environment.
> - We can practise being friendly/polite at any time.

3. **Do:** Display the cards in an area in the room.

Movement: Bucket Filling

Aims

- To teach children the concept of being "bucket fillers", i.e., being kind and thoughtful to others.

Materials

- A bucket.
- Colourful small objects (that can be placed into a bucket).
- Uplifting music (optional).

Instructions

1. **Explain:** A bucket can represent how we feel about ourselves – when our bucket is full, we are more likely to feel friendly, confident, calm, and positive. However, when our bucket is empty, we are more likely to feel sad, unconfident, and worried. We can help fill each other's buckets by becoming "bucket fillers".
2. **Ask:** What could we do to fill another person's bucket and help them feel good? What might empty their bucket?

> **Key Messages to Share**
>
> - How to fill a bucket, e.g., doing or saying something kind or thoughtful that shows you care; helping others; smiling at each other; being polite and respectful.
> - How to empty a bucket, e.g., doing or saying unkind things; teasing; cruel words; being unhelpful; being impolite and disrespectful.

3. **Do:** Have the children form a circle around the bucket. Have them skip around the bucket until the music stops (or until you say "stop"). Have each child (one at a time) move to the bucket to pick it up. Ask the rest of the group to say something kind and thoughtful about that child and then place a colourful object in the bucket in order to fill his/her bucket. You may also like to ask the child with the bucket to share a kind word about him/herself.

> **Note**
>
> - You may like to have pictures and/or words that could be placed in the bucket by the other children.

> **Modification Suggestions for 3-year-old Group**
>
> * You may want to get each student to decorate the bucket as well.
> * You may prepare some concrete objects made with felt materials with which students can fill the bucket, e.g., smiling sun, a helping hand, an angry dragon.

Topic 4: Empathic Sharing (E)

Sharing is caring ... it is important to listen to how other children are feeling

(Quote from a group of pre-school children)

Early Years Situation Card: Choosing a Group to Play With

Aims

- To learn how to share with others.
- To understand the impact of sharing and not sharing with others.

The day when we had excursions and three specialist classes, we were in the middle of the sharing and caring lesson. Instead of doing it in class, I asked the children to go into the playground and collect one little thing for each other so that we could exchange it secretly. It is COPE-R in action.

Materials

- Early Years Situation Card "Choosing a Group to Play With".
- Alternatives: Images from Appendix 2 or other substitutes.

Instructions

1. **Explain:** Playing and sharing with others helps develop friendships. If we don't share with another, the other person may feel sad and we could miss out on fun times together.
2. **Do:** Show the children the Situation Card "Choosing a Group to Play With".

Figure 16 "Choosing a Group to Play With" Situation Card".

Implementation of COPE-R

3. **Ask:**

   - What is happening in this picture?
   - What are some sharing behaviours shown in this picture?
   - What do you think each child is feeling? How would you feel in this situation?
   - What would be some non-sharing behaviours in this situation?
   - How could the boy play with both groups of children, so that he is sharing his time?
   - Has this situation ever happened to you? What did you do?

   Key Messages to Share

   - The two boys are sharing a ball with one another (if they were not sharing, one child may be keeping the ball to himself).
   - The two girls are sharing a tea party together (if they were not sharing, the tea party would only be for one child, which wouldn't be a party at all!).
   - Not sharing or not including others in play can make others unhappy and we may miss out on learning a new game/activity and having fun.
   - The boy could play with both groups of children by taking turns playing; he could ask the boys if he could play ball, and then ask the girls if he could join their tea party.

Feelings Explorer: How Can We Share

Aims

- To understand that sharing is not just about sharing tangible items.
- To learn about other ways to share with others.

When we celebrated Indigenous languages week, we incorporated a specific custom of the Wurundjeri people of giving bouquets to friends and using specific flowers to indicate either love or friendship.

Materials

- Flipchart paper and markers.

Instructions

1. **Explain:** Did you know that we can share in many different ways. It is about sharing our belongings and it is also about sharing our thoughts and ideas.
2. **Ask:** If you had no belongings to share with someone, what could you share instead?
3. **Do:** On the flipchart paper, note the ideas generated. Suggest to the children to do one of these sharing acts today/this week, etc.

Key Messages to Share

- Examples of other ways to share: sharing smiles, sharing a hug, sharing ideas/stories, sharing a kind thought with someone, sharing your friends, sharing the play equipment, spending the day with someone, listening to someone, sharing a chore with someone, dancing together, singing together, calling a family member you don't speak to often, sharing flowers, making someone breakfast/lunch.
- Learning to share in different ways allows us to give to another even when we may not have tangible items to share.

Note

- You may like to ask the children: if you had no money, how could you give/share with another instead of buying something?

Role-play: Tricky Sharing Situations

Aims

- To learn how to problem solve situations that involve difficulties with sharing.
- To practise appropriate ways of sharing.

It's actually as simple as this. "You are two friends with the same problem, and we need to solve it. You need to understand each other". Once you sort the problem, the group actually goes back to work in a really focused way and it doesn't feel like an interruption because they know that once the problem is resolved they are more focused and more into whatever they were doing.

Materials

- A special object that is popular with the children.
- A poster with the words: STOP/THINK/DO.

Preparation

- Remind children about friendly and polite behaviours learnt previously as many of these relate to sharing.

Instructions

1. **Do:** Show children the special object.
2. **Explain:** Many of you like to play with something special, and sometimes there are disagreements and conflicts about who is going to play with it. If we are unsure about how we can share we can be problem solvers by using STOP/THINK/DO. [Show poster]. STOP means that you tell yourself to stop what you are doing, THINK about appropriate friendly/polite/sharing behaviours, and finally recognise and DO the appropriate behaviour.
3. **Ask:** What are some ideas for sharing a special object in a friendly and polite way? If we are unable to play with it, what could we do other than getting upset?

Key Messages to Share

- Examples of sharing: taking turns; swapping; playing together; waiting patiently; asking politely/in a nice way; using expressions such as: "may I?", "can I?", "could I?"; responding politely/in a nice way.
- Being problem solvers means thinking about solutions, so that everyone is happy.
- Rather than getting upset, we can find something else to do/play.
- If you do not want to share a special item from home, it may be better to leave it in your bag.
- "We need to make wise choices so we can stay safe and so nobody gets hurt" (quote from a group of pre-school children).

4. **Do:** With the whole class observing, role-play a scenario (e.g., where two children both want to play with the object) while using the STOP/THINK/DO strategy. After the whole group exercise, organise children into pairs or small groups to practise the STOP/THINK/DO strategy and appropriate sharing behaviours using different scenarios.

Examples of Other Scenarios

- Wanting to use a particular coloured pen at the same time as another child.
- Giving a friend one of your special items, e.g., a necklace, to have for the day but who doesn't want to give it back to you at the end of day.
- Wanting to play in the cubby house with your friend; however, other children are already there.
- Playing a ball game with your friend who then takes the ball away to play by him/herself.
- Looking at a book when another child wants to have a look too.
- Your friend wants the special treat in your lunchbox, which you have been looking forward to eating.

Note

- Rather than solving the problem for the children, reinforce the STOP/THINK/DO strategy and explore possible solutions with them.

Modification Suggestions for 3-year-old Group

* You may wish to prepare a STOP/THINK/DO traffic light poster to illustrate the concept.

Art: We Share a Life

Aims

- To learn that we are all part of a community and we can share with each other and our lives.
- To identify a variety of ways of sharing other than using tangible items.

Materials

- Flipchart paper and pencil.
- Piece of paper for each child.
- Pencils/crayons.

Instructions

1. **Explain:** Let's think about sharing. There are lots of different ways to share. We can share items such as toys. We can share our thoughts, feelings, and ideas. We can also share our lives and ourselves with others in the community.
2. **Ask:**

    - What are some <u>items</u> we can share?
    - What are some <u>thoughts, feelings, and ideas</u> we can share?
    - What can we do to care for <u>the community</u>?

3. **Do:** On the flipchart paper, note examples under the headings of "items", "ideas", and "community".

> **Key Messages to Share**
>
> - Examples of items: toys, pens and pencils, food.
> - Examples of thoughts, feelings, and ideas: "I think you are lovely", "I appreciate you", "I think we could build this Lego man by using these Lego blocks".
> - Examples of caring for the community: taking care of the environment, e.g., no littering; being kind to people we meet; taking care of others.

4. **Explain:** I would like you to draw something that you could share with others. It can be an item, an idea, or doing something for the community.
5. **Do:** Display the drawings around the room with a description of what each child has drawn.

Optional Activity

Movement: Creating a Sharing Poem/Song

Aims

- To create a poem/song as a group that involves sharing and listening to everyone's ideas.
- To extend understandings of sharing behaviours through language, e.g., poems, songs, riddles.

Materials

- Flipchart paper and pencil.

Preparation

- It is recommended that this activity is implemented after the other activities, so that children have some understanding and vocabulary about sharing.

Instructions

1. **Explain:** Together we are going to write a poem/song about sharing. Firstly we need to write some words that describe sharing.
2. **Ask:** What does sharing involve? How do we feel when we share? What can we share?

> **Key Messages to Share**
>
> - Sharing involves a range of behaviours, e.g., taking turns; swapping; playing together; waiting patiently; asking politely/in a nice way; using expressions such as: "may I?", "can I?", "could I?"; responding politely.
> - When we share, we feel happy, good, lovely, beautiful, proud, friendly, caring, and loving. It is a nice thing to do and helps develop friendships. If we do not share, our friends may think that we do not care about them, that we are selfish/mean, and that we do not want to play with them.
> - We can share tangible and non-tangible items, e.g., sharing a smile, hug, ideas.

3. **Do:** Write the children's ideas on the flipchart paper. Begin to create a very simple poem that incorporates these ideas, e.g., sharing is caring; we love sharing; share with me. Example of a song created by a 4-year-old girl to cheer up her friend: *We are happy furry foxes, on our claws we put our sockses, and we go to the forest shopses, to buy some delicious mushroom-moxes.*

Implementation of COPE-R

Optional Activity

Feelings Explorer: Understanding Others

Aims

- To understand that others may not always think or feel the way you do.
- To learn about other people's feelings

We talked about President X and then a child said, "oh yes, he is horrible, I wish he could die" and then another child said, "do you know that the President is a dad" and then everyone just stopped straight away. The other child says, "what would happen if you kill someone's dad" and then it really turned; it flipped the whole conversation upside down seeing that person, not as a President, but just as a normal person living an everyday life just like they are.

Materials

Books that touch on aspects of empathy and perspective taking, e.g.

- *Voices in the Park* by Anthony Browne (best suited for children aged 5–7).
- *Sometimes I Feel Sunny* by Gillian Shields and Georgie Birkett (best suited for children aged 2–5).

Instructions

4. **Explain:** Did you know that we don't always feel the same way as each other? Sometimes when we are feeling happy, someone else might be feeling sad. That is okay, and we can learn how others are feeling.
5. **Do:** Read the storybook to a class.
6. **Ask:**

- What do you think is happening to the character?
- What feelings do the characters have? Have you experienced this before?
- What did the character do to help manage the feelings? What else would you do that might be helpful?

Key Messages to Share

- There is no wrong way to feel.
- It is important to think about how others feel.
- You can ask how other people feel if you are not sure.

Optional Activity
Feelings Explorer: Helping Others Feel Better

Aims

- To work together to brainstorm ideas around how to help others feel better.
- To extend understanding of sharing and caring behaviours with others.

Materials

- Flipchart paper and pencil.

Preparation

- It is recommended that this activity be implemented after the other activities, so that children have some understanding and vocabulary about sharing and caring.

Instructions

4. **Explain:** Together we are going to come up with a list of things we can do to help others feel better.
5. **Ask:** How do you know how someone else feels?
   Possible answers: Listen to what they say, ask them how they feel, look closely at their face and body, watch what they do.
6. **Ask:** How can we recognise when another child is feeling bad or left out?
   Possible answers: See if they are making a sad face, not laughing when others laugh, crying, not looking at anyone, playing alone.
7. **Ask:** How can we help children who feel bad to feel better?
   Possible answers: Pay attention to them, sit with them, pat them on the back, ask them if they would like to play with you.

Key Messages to Share

- It's important to check how other people are feeling if they look upset.
- We can help by asking how they feel, and offering our help.

Note

- You may like to ask the children: if you felt sad, what would you like someone else to do for you to help you feel better?

Topic 5: Review (R)

Overview of the Review Session

The purpose of the review sessions is to reinforce the core principles of the COPE-R program: namely, caring, kindness, emotional understanding, sharing of emotions, and open communication. A landmark study followed 800 people for their lifetime to see what actually makes people live longer, healthier, and happier; it found six key factors that impact happiness and longevity, including relationships, education, and generosity. In the adult world it is about generativity, which is community building, having friends and relationships, and having coping skills (Waldinger, 2007). In early childhood it is about developing the principles of caring, sharing, and empathy, and the ability to build relationships and develop healthy coping skills. We can communicate in silence by taking notice of all that is around us. It is often not the noisemaker who should be noticed but rather the quiet, caring individual who acknowledges the feelings of others. Finally, resilience can be built through a range of activities such as a walk through the forest where challenges can be found in the everyday environment.

Aim

For the children and teacher to review learning from the previous four sessions and cross-reference new knowledge across all areas of the curriculum.

Learning experiences

- Create a bank of words that communicate care, concern, and empathy.
- Ask children to choose the word that resonates with them the most and write this word on a name tag with string to hang on "care and respect tree".
- Host a Japanese Tea Ceremony where the sharing of care, open communication, politeness, and empathy are enacted.
- Create a poster for the children to display, so as to remind them about the importance of caring and sharing the space.
- Sing songs that celebrate friendship, kindness, and caring.
- Share final thoughts as a celebration of new knowledge and understandings.

Feelings Explorer: The Caring Tree

Aims

- For children to identify what they have learnt from the program.
- For children to share their experiences with the whole class.

Materials

- Paper tags.
- An object that can be used to hang paper tags, e.g., branches from a tree.
- Pens.

Preparation

- Create your Caring Tree and ensure the paper tags are an appropriate size to enable easeful decoration of the tree.

Instructions

1. **Explain:** Over the past few weeks we have been learning about caring, communication, politeness/friendliness, and sharing. I want you to write your word on a paper tag. Once we have all finished, we are going to share our words with the whole group and then place them on our Caring Tree.
2. **Do:** Assist any children who are having difficulties generating and/or writing a word.
3. **Do:** Help each child hang their paper tag on the Caring Tree.

> **Key Message to Share**
>
> - Examples of words for the Caring Tree: sharing, love yourself, friends; playing together, humans care, people I love, listening, kindness, respect.

> **Note**
>
> - You may like the children to add to the Caring Tree throughout the year as they learn more words about the topics addressed in the program.

Feelings Explorer: Kind Acts

Aims

- For each child to identify a kind act s/he has done for another during the program.

Materials

- Notepad, etc., to write the children's responses.

Instructions

1. **Do:** Have the children sit in a circle on the floor.
2. **Explain:** We have been learning about the importance of caring for others, which includes being kind and nice to others. As we move around the circle, I want you to share with the rest of the group one kind act you have done for someone – this could have been for a friend, family member, educator, etc.
3. **Do:** Have each child share their kind act and note their responses. Ensure educators also contribute to the discussion. At the end of the activity, review the kind acts by reading the children's examples to the group, and discuss how kind/thoughtful actions show care for others.

Key Messages to Share

- Examples of kind acts: doing a drawing for your brother/sister; giving a friend a hug/kiss; writing a friendship card; saying something nice to someone; telling someone, "I love you"; holding a friend's hand and inviting them to play when s/he is feeling sad; sharing your favourite toy with a friend; sharing ideas when working together on an activity; sharing a book; asking your friend to play.
- Kind acts are like "hugs that keep you warm".

Note

- You may want to ask the children to draw these kind acts and display them in the room.

Modification Suggestions for 3-year-old Group

* You may bring out the bucket again and have the bucket filled each time an act of kindness is shared.

Role-play: Sharing From One Teapot

Aims

- To introduce the children to the Japanese Tea Ceremony and the rituals surrounding the sharing of tea in a social setting.
- To revisit the concepts of sharing and listening and the notion of silence during a tea party.
- To practise effective communication skills such as good listening.

Materials

- One teapot and herbal tea.
- Aesthetically pleasing tablecloth and vase of fresh flowers.
- One small table with a few chairs.
- Multiple teacups and saucers.

Preparation

- Set up a tea party on a table.
- Make a brew of herbal tea.

Instructions

1. **Explain:** We have been learning about sharing and there are many activities we can share with others, such as playing together and having a "tea party".
2. **Ask:** [Point to the table]. Someone tell me how we can share when having a tea party?

> **Key Messages to Share**
>
> - We can share by using the same teapot and by taking it in turns to pour tea.
> - Having a tea party can be a quiet and relaxing time shared with others. We can also share stories and laughs, talk to old friends, and make new friends.
> - A tea party also requires the use of polite and respectful language with each other, listening to others when they talk, and allowing others to contribute to the conversation.

3. **Do:** Choose a group of children to visit the tea party table to experience sharing a social activity. Ensure all children have the opportunity to participate in this activity in small groups. Visit each group to discuss what they have shared and how they are feeling.

> **Note**
>
> - You may like to use this activity as an opportunity for children to make new friends.

Art: Hunting and Gathering for Pleasant Feelings

Aims

- To identify times when we have felt happy and relaxed and to name different positive/pleasant feelings.

Materials

- Large pieces of paper that can be made into a newspaper.
- Pencils/crayons.

Instructions

1. **Explain:** We have been learning about feelings and the different names for them.
2. **Ask:** What are some positive/pleasant feelings?

> **Key Message to Share**
>
> - Examples of positive feelings: happy, excited, funny, proud, cheerful, loving, kind, strong, grateful, surprise, confident, enjoyment, playful, courageous, curious.

3. **Explain:** We are going to create our own newspaper! Firstly, we are going to be hunters and gatherers of positive/pleasant feelings so that this newspaper will be about the times when you have experienced these feelings. I want each of you to draw a time when you felt happy. We will then put all these drawings together to make a newspaper, and I will write your "news" story underneath your drawing.
4. **Do**: Assist children to identify times when they felt happy. Collect all the drawings, ensure a story has been written for each of the drawings, and bind them together to create a newspaper. Discuss with the children an appropriate title for the newspaper.

Art: Sending Caring Messages Around the World

Aims

- To review how to care for others by what we say and what we do.
- To become world "messengers" of caring.

Materials

- A large piece of paper cut to look like a postage stamp.
- Pencils/crayons.

Instructions

1. **Explain:** We have been learning about the many ways we can care for others. By caring for others, we not only help someone feel good but we can also feel good about ourselves. What are some caring acts? What type of caring acts have you done for others?

   ### Key Message to Share

   - Examples of caring acts: give someone a hug, say something nice to someone, help someone, listen to others when they are talking, play with others, help feed and walk the dog, water the plants.

2. **Explain:** We are going to create a large postage stamp. A postage stamp is used when sending letters/messages to others around the world. What message could we put on our postage stamp to show everyone around the world how to care for others?

   ### Key Message to Share

   - Examples of messages: caring is sharing, caring means being nice to others, say kind words to each other, look after one another, love one another, respect and protect the environment, be kind to animals.

3. **Do:** As the children provide examples write them on the prepared blank postage stamp. Once completed, review the messages with the children and have them colour in/draw on the stamp.

   ### Note

   - You may like to have the children create their own postage stamp to place on an envelope and to also include in the envelope one of their drawings from the program.

Implementation of COPE-R

Optional Activity
Art: COPE-Resilience Game

Aims

- To create (or play) a fun game that encompasses the themes of COPE-R (i.e., caring, open communication, politeness, empathic sharing).

Materials

- Pieces of paper/cardboard.
- Pencils/crayons.

Instructions

1. **Explain:** Over the past few weeks we have been learning about caring, open communication, politeness/friendliness, and sharing. We are going to make a fun game to practise the skills we have learnt.

> **Key Message to Share**
>
> - Examples of games to make: a board game with activities to show caring, politeness, and sharing; a charade like game where children have to guess the caring and kind act being acted out; a game of SNAP where the cards have words/pictures reflecting themes from COPE-R.

2. **Do:** Assist the children in developing and designing the game and play the game in small groups or as a whole class (if appropriate). Encourage listening to one another, turn taking, exchanging of ideas, and negotiating and sharing.

Optional Activity
Movement: Creating a Mandala of Silence

Aims

- To review the importance of listening to others.
- To understand the usefulness of silence to listen better to others.

Materials

- A voice chart displaying a colour key to identify different voice levels (i.e., 0 to 5, where 0 = absolute silence (white); 3 = normal conversation voice (yellow); 5 = playground voice (red). For more information refer back to Voice Chart.
- A collection of different coloured stones or small pieces of paper.
- A large piece of paper with the title, "mandala of silence", or "Where can silence be found?"

Instructions

1. **Explain:** We have been learning about how to talk with one another and the importance of listening with our heart when others speak to us.
2. **Ask:** What is important when we listen to each other? How could we be better listeners?

> **Key Messages to Share**
>
> - Listening can sometimes be difficult if there is a lot of noise indoors and/or outdoors.
> - Maybe we can be better listeners if we go to places where "silence can be found". We can then hear what others are saying a lot better and learn more about each other.
> - Listening to others also involves looking at the person when they are talking.

3. **Explain:** We are going to create a "mandala of silence" and use coloured stones/paper to identify the level of sounds in different places. On this table is a piece of paper. I want each of you to think of a place or sound that is quiet and move to the table to place appropriate coloured stone/papers to represent how quiet this place/sound is.
4. **Do:** Provide an example for the children, e.g., under a tree where there are a few children playing. On the paper, place white stones (to represent times when it can be very quiet), yellow stones (to represent soft sounds when birds may be chirping), and blue stones (to represent medium sounds when children are talking nearby).
5. **Ask:** Discuss with each child where their quiet place is or what sound they have chosen and write their example next to their stones (see following picture as an example).

Implementation of COPE-R

Below shows an example of a mandala of silence created by a group of children.

Figure 17 Mandala of silence.

Key Message to Share

- Examples of quiet places/sounds: in the trees, quiet music, under mushrooms, in my heart, inside the flowers, in a possum's nest, in the forest, under the bed, gum trees, in the doona, in water, in the garden, in my bedroom, inside a rose.

Note

- You may like to spend a few minutes being silent/quiet as a group when sitting in a circle.

Implementation of COPE-R

Activity Example from a Teacher's Adaptation

Creating a mandala of silence

Context: A group of children were encouraged to carefully choose one object of special interest, from the basket (chosen for their silent property) and gently put it in their own mandala of silence (see the following picture as an example).

Figure 18 Children creating a silence mandala.

Example of objects:

- Feather – it makes a soft sound or no sound at all.
- Cocoon – silkworm's house, always silent.
- Corals – they sway softly and quietly.
- Pin cushion – it reminds of own pillow.

Optional Activity

Mix and Match: Creating and Understanding Facial Expressions

Aims

- To review identification and understanding of feelings through expressions and perspective taking.
- To reinforce the importance of showing empathetic responses to others.

Materials

- A template of a human face.
- Facial features of eyebrows, eyes, nose, and mouth.

Instructions

1. **Explain:** We have been learning about how to identify and understand the feelings of others. We also learnt ways to show kindness to others who are feeling upset. We are going to mix and match the eyebrows, eyes, nose, and mouth to make a facial expression. Then, you will imitate the facial expressions created and share a situation that will make you feel that way.
2. **Do:** Provide an example for the children, e.g., select slanted eyebrows, big round eyes, high nose, and open mouth, then imitate the facial expression and ask what this feeling is (scared).
3. **Ask:** Discuss with the children about the feeling and come up with a situation that might trigger this feeling. Then, discuss some empathetic responses that can be shown to someone who is feeling scared, e.g., "what can you do?" and "what can you say?"
4. **Do:** Children will then take turns to share and suggest empathetic responses.

Implementation of COPE-R

Optional Activity

Rites of Passage: Training Resilience

Aims

- To review and reinforce the importance of coping and resilience.
- To practise productive coping strategies and to support one another.

Instructions

1. **Explain:** We have been learning about how to cope with challenging situations. We learnt to care and support others who are feeling down or hurt. Now, we are all going for a nature walk. We are going to help each other and finish the walk together.
2. **Do:** Take the class to a walking track that poses some challenge, e.g., a steep incline. The location will depend on the situation of your organisation. Take this opportunity to encourage children to endure challenges and support one another. Educators may like to take photos of the children to facilitate discussion later.
3. **Ask:** Following the completion of the walk, discuss with the children about how they felt during the walk and what they observed in other children. You may also like to discuss what the children can do when they see their friends feeling tired and wanting to give up, as well as how they feel when they support their peers or are being supported by their peers.
4. **Do:** Children will then take turns to share their responses. Pictures of children, e.g., facial expressions, success in completing the walk, empathetic responses, can be presented to the children to help guide the discussion and review the key concepts learnt.

v A teacher's experience and reflection on COPE-R

Over the six years, an experienced pre-school teacher from the ELC community has committed to implementing the COPE-R program with various groups of pre-school children. We have gathered their insights throughout the years and presented below their suggestions for implementation and also their personal reflections.

- *What is it that makes this classroom feel like I'm on a holiday? We really look after each other, and we are not the best of friends, we are colleagues. The constant support and constant dealing with issues, not just the children's, actually help us deal with our own issues when we have something. I am using COPE-R sentences and strategies with my own friends. I realise that I am coping by finding joy and fun in this as well. And I think the children get it on that level as well.*

- *It's actually really helping and enhancing the cognitive process of teaching. The skills that I've probably developed the most is the skill of awareness and listening skills. We used to deal with the situation at the end of the day when the parents arrived to collect the specific child or after the class or after the specific lesson. But with COPE-R there's this awareness that you see the teachable moment immediately so we are actually stopping whatever we are doing at the very point when something happens. For example, when there is an outburst or aggression or something, together as a group we deal with that straight away and we keep the coping language in focus as well.*

- *Each day brings something new ... when we are doing COPE-R, we are doing it over weeks but [the program] goes longer because it's constantly present in the classroom. You can see the child being unpolite, you can see who is expressing empathy towards another. It is like you've developed this sixth sense of what's going on in the classroom through a COPE-R lens you see what you didn't see before. Every time an opportunity arises, we stop and look at that very specific thing that just happened in the classroom and try to incorporate COPE-R activities, knowledge, and reflections straight away. It has become more and more meaningful each year. As a teacher I keep adding my own elements and just fit them into the curriculum as I go. I would never go through a year without having COPE-R.*

vi Supplementary materials for educators/facilitators/teachers

> *I constantly go back to my journal to reflect on it. What works well and what can be improved and what can I repeat.*

The reflective questions below are designed to help you to process the experience of implementing COPE-R with your own group of pre-schoolers. You can do this after each lesson or as a weekly reflective activity.

- What are your best hopes for trialling COPE-R with your group of children?
- What differences would you notice if your group of children is progressing?
- How do you plan and implement the COPE-R activities that engage children and promote social emotional learning?
- How do you use effective verbal and non-verbal communication strategies to support children's understanding of, participation in, and engagement with each of the topic areas of COPE-R?
- What strategies have you used to promote a safe environment in your setting to encourage children to practise and use the prosocial skills taught in COPE-R?
- What resources have been helpful to you to create visual reminders for children on key topic areas within your setting?
- What informal and formal assessment strategies have you developed or used to assess children's learning after each COPE-R lesson?
- How do you provide timely, effective, and appropriate feedback to children about their behaviour and actions in relation to each of the COPE-R domains?
- What personal and professional learnings have you undertaken to deepen your understanding on social emotional development?
- What changes have you noticed in yourself through this journey?
- Who else can you partner with to continue making progress on this journey?

Program background references

Allison, C., Baron-Cohen, S., Wheelwright, S. J., Stone, M. H., & Muncer, S. J. (2011). Psychometric analysis of the Empathy Quotient (EQ). *Personality and Individual Differences, 51*(7), 829–835.

Bailey, C. S., Rivers, S. E., Tominey, S. L., O'Bryon, E. C., Olsen, S. G., Sneeden, C. K., ... Brackett, M. A. (2019). *Promoting Early Childhood Social and Emotional Learning with Preschool RULER*. Manuscript submitted for publication, Yale Child Study Center, Yale School of Medicine.

Bain, J., James, D., & Harrison, M. (2015). Supporting communication development in the early years: A practitioner's perspective. *Child Language Teaching & Therapy, 31*(3), 325–336. doi:10.1177/0265659015596795.

Baron-Cohen, S., & Wheelwright, S. (2004). The empathy quotient: An investigation of adults with Asperger syndrome or high functioning autism, and normal sex differences. *Journal of Autism and Developmental Disorders, 34*(2), 163–175.

Bowlby, J. (1969). *Attachment and loss, Vol. 1: Attachment*. Basic Books.

Brackett, M. (2019). *Permission to feel: Unlocking the power of emotions to help our kids, ourselves, and our society thrive*. Celadon Books.

Brackett, M. A., Rivers, S. E., Reyes, M. R., & Salovey, P. (2012). Enhancing academic performance and social and emotional competence with the RULER feeling words curriculum. *Learning and Individual Differences, 22*(2), 218–224. doi:10.1016/j.lindif.2010.10.002.

Bronfenbrenner, U. (1979). *The ecology of human development: Experiments by nature and design*. Harvard University Press.

Bronfenbrenner, U. (1994). Ecological models of human development. *International encyclopedia of education* (vol. 3, 2nd.ed), Elsevier.

Center on the Developing Child at Harvard University. (2020, April 30). *InBrief: executive function: Skills for life and learning*. https://developingchild.harvard.edu/resources/inbrief-executive-function-skills-for-life-and-learning/

Cornell, C., Kiernan, N., Kaufman, D., Dobeee, P., Frydenberg, E., & Deans, J. (2017). Developing social emotional competence in the early years. In E. Frydenberg, A. J. Martin, & R. J. Collie (Eds.), *Social and emotional learning in Australia and the Asia-Pacific* (pp. 391–441). Springer.

Deans, J., Frydenberg, E., & Tsurutani, H. (2010). Operationalising social and emotional coping competencies in kindergarten children. *New Zealand Research In Early Childhood Education, 13*, 113–124.

Deans, J., Klarin, S., Liang, R., & Frydenberg, E. (2017). All children have the best start in life to create a better future for themselves and for the nation. *Australasian Journal of Early Childhood, 4*, 78.

Deans, J., Liang, R., & Frydenberg, E. (2016, March 1). Giving voices and providing skills to families in culturally and linguistically diverse communities through a productive parenting program. *Australasian Journal of Early Childhood, 41*, 13–18.

Decety, J. (2011). The neuroevolution of empathy. *Annals of the New York Academy of Sciences*, *1231*, 35–45.

Denham, S. A., Bassett, H. H., & Miller, S. L. (2017). Early childhood teachers' socialization of emotion: Contextual and individual contributors. *Child & Youth Care Forum*, *46*(6), 805–824.

Denham, S. A., & Burton, R. (2003). *Social and emotional prevention and intervention programming for pre-schoolers*. Kluwer Academic/Plenum Publishers.

Eisenberg, N., Fabes, R. A., & Spinrad, T. L. (2006). Prosocial development. In W. Damon & R. Lerner (Eds..), *Handbook of child psychology, social, emotional, and personality development* (vol. 3, pp. 646–702). John Wiley & Sons.

Feshbach, N. D. (1982). Sex differences in empathy and social behavior in children. In N. Eisenberg (Ed.), *The development of prosocial behavior* (pp. 315–338). Academic Press.

Feshbach, N. D., & Feshbach, S. (2009). Empathy and education. In J. Decety & W. Ickes (Eds.), *The social neuroscience of empathy* (pp. 85–98). The MIT Press.

Frydenberg, E. (2015). *Families coping: Effective strategies for you and your child*. Australian Council for Educational Research (ACER Press.).

Frydenberg, E. (2017). *Coping and the challenge of resilience*. Palgrave Macmillan.

Frydenberg, E., & Deans, J. (2011). *The early years coping cards*. Australian Council for Educational Research (ACER Press.).

Frydenberg, E., Deans, J., & Liang, R. (2020). *Promoting well-being in the pre-school years*. Routledge.

Frydenberg, E., Deans, J., & O'Brien, K. (2012). *Developing everyday coping skills in the early years: Proactive strategies for supporting social and emotional development*. Continuum Inc. Press.

Fugelsnes, K. (2018). Reciprocal caring in ECEC settings. In E. Johansson, A. Emilson, & A.-M. Puroila (Eds..), *Values education in early childhood settings: Concepts, approaches and practices* (pp. 187–198). Springer.

Huebscher, I., Garufi, M., & Prieto, P. (2019). The development of polite stance in preschoolers: How prosody, gesture, and body cues pave the way. *Journal Of Child Language*, *46*(5), 825–862. doi:10.1017/S0305000919000126.

Ma, X., Tamir, M., & Miyamoto, Y. (2017). A socio-cultural instrumental approach to emotion regulation. *Culture and the Regulation of Positive Emotions. Emotion*, *18*, 138–152. doi:10.1037/emo0000315.

Mayer, J. D., Roberts, R. D., & Barsade, S. G. (2008). Human abilities: Emotional intelligence. *Annual Review of Psychology*, *59*, 507–536.

Mayer, J. D., & Salovey, P. (1993). The intelligence of emotional intelligence. *Intelligence*, *17*, 433–442.

McLean, S. (2016). *The effect of trauma on the brain development of children: evidence-based principles for supporting the recovery of children in care (CFCA practitioner resource)*. Melbourne: Child Family Community Australia information exchange, Australian Institute of Family Studies.

Nakamura, K. (2006). The acquisition of linguistic politeness in Japanese. In M. Nakayama, R. Mazuka, & Y. Shirai (Eds.), *The handbook of East Asian psycholinguistics: Volume II Japanese* (pp. 110–115). Cambridge University Press.

Ornaghi, V., Pepe, A., & Grazzani, I. (2016). False-belief understanding and language ability mediate the relationship between emotion comprehension and prosocial orientation in preschoolers. *Frontiers in Psychology*, *7*, 1534. doi:10.3389/fpsyg.2016.01534.

Pang, D., Frydenberg, E., Liang, R., & Deans, J. (2018). Improving coping skills & promoting social and emotional competence in pre-schoolers: A 5-week COPE-R program. *Journal of Early Childhood Education Research*, 7(2), 1–31.

Pedlow, R., Sanson, A., & Wales, R. (2004). Children's production and comprehension of politeness in requests: Relationships to behavioural adjustment, temperament and empathy. *First Language, 24*(3), 347–367.

Petersen, L., & Adderley, A. (2002). *STOP THINK DO social skills training: Early years of schooling ages 4-8*. ACER Press.

Piaget, J. (1952). *The origins of intelligence in children*. Norton & Co.

Salovey, P., & Mayer, J. D. (1990). Emotional intelligence. *Imagination, Cognition, and Personality, 9*, 185–211.

Schwenck, C., Göhle, B., Hauf, J., Warnke, A., Freitag, C. M., & Schneider, W. (2014). Cognitive and emotional empathy in typically developing children: The influence of age, gender, and intelligence. *European Journal of Developmental Psychology, 11*(1), 63–76. doi:https://doi.org/10.1080/17405629.2013.808994.

Seligman, M. E. P., Ernst, R., Gillham, J., Reivich, K., & Linkins, M. (2009). Positive education: Positive psychology and classroom interventions. *Oxford Review of Education, 35*, 293–311.

Smith, C. A. (2013). Beyond "I'm sorry": The educator's role in preschoolers' emergence of conscience. *Young Children, 68*(1), 76.

Vygotsky, L. (1962). *Thought and language*. MIT Press.

White, M. A., & Waters, L. E. (2015). A case study of 'The Good School:' Examples of the use of Peterson's strengths-based approach with students. *The Journal of Positive Psychology, 10*(1), 69–76.

Wu, M. Y., Alexander, M. A., Frydenberg, E., & Deans, J. (2019). *Teacher experience matters: Social emotional learning in the early years*. Australian Educational Researchers.

Appendix 1: Mindfulness and relaxation[1]

Mindfulness in simple terms means focusing one's attention on the present moment, without judging it as good or bad. By doing so, we are expanding our awareness to directly experience life as it is. It is something that we all naturally possess and can be strengthened by regular practice. Please note that the mindfulness and relaxation exercises below are provided as suggestions only. You are encouraged to adapt these activities (e.g., format, language) to be age-appropriate for the children.

Mindfulness of senses (e.g., savouring food)

Take a sultana, a jellybean, a grape, or a small piece of chocolate. Notice the texture, the smell of it, and then slowly explore it as you put it in your mouth. Savour the taste, texture, and enjoyment before finally swallowing it.

Mindfulness of body (e.g., breathing, listening to sounds)

This exercise is best done with eyes closed in a setting that is pleasant and distraction free. It is also helpful to sit comfortably on the ground with legs crossed. The outdoors provides an opportunity to listen and hear a wide range of sounds. In this activity you are encouraged to be conscious of your breathing, to make it comfortable, not too long and not too short. Following a focus on breathing, you are then encouraged to listen for sounds and smells in the environment. Following the activity, you are invited to have a conversation or reflect on the experience. How easy or difficult was it to focus on breathing alone, sounds and smells and how enjoyable was the experience?

Adults can guide children through a similar or adapted activity. Mindfulness activities have been written for adults but children can be readily led through an adapted activity.

Mindfulness of self (e.g., identifying emotions in the body)

In this exercise you are encouraged to identify emotions, such as happiness, sadness, excitement, anxiety, anger, calmness, and so on, and where each of these emotions are being experienced. You are encouraged just to observe the emotion, identify its location, and accept it without judgment. However, if you or a child frequently experiences a particular emotion, especially if it is troublesome, then there can be a focus on that emotion.

---

1 Adapted from Frydenberg, 2015.

Appendix 1: Mindfulness and relaxation

Relaxation (Time: 15–30 minutes)

This is a frequently used exercise to encourage relaxation. As with the *mindfulness of body* activity, you are encouraged to be seated in a comfortable position, on the floor with legs uncrossed or on a chair with legs uncrossed and arms relaxed and hanging comfortably, open palms, and relaxed fingers.

> You can start the relaxation exercise from the toes upwards or from the head downwards. If you are starting at the lower extremity, you will first focus on your toes and feel the sensation in them, notice the feeling, and relax the toes. You then follow through by relaxing the sole of your feet, the ankles, the calves, the knees, and the thighs. You can first do this with the right foot and right leg and then the left foot and the left leg. Breathe all the time gently in and out. You can then follow up with your upper body, noticing each inner organ, one at a time – for example the stomach, the chest, the rib cage, lungs, and so on. In a similar fashion, you can move from the extremities of the right finger and hand through to the right shoulder and then do likewise with the left hand, through the left arm to the left shoulder. The neck and upper part of the shoulder and head are often sources of stress and discomfort. You are encouraged to focus carefully on the lower part of the neck, moving upwards through the various elements of the face such as the chin, mouth, cheeks, nose, eyes, and forehead. This exercise can take from 15 to 30 minutes and is practised by some people on a regular basis.

Appendix 2: Situation and coping images[1] for personal use

Situation Cards 1

Broken Toy

Worry Leaving

Fear of Dark

In Trouble

Broken Toy 2

Bullied Teased

1 Artwork by Jock Macneish at Strategic Images: www.strategicimages.com.au

Appendix 2: Situation and coping images for personal use

Situation Cards 2

Losing Something

Afraid of New

Want to Belong

Getting Hurt

Coping Cards 1

Play

Hug a Toy

Think

Cry

Happy Thoughts

Blame Others

Help Others

Help Share

Appendix 2: Situation and coping images for personal use

Coping Cards 2

 Blame Self

 Work Hard

 Tantrum

 Keep Private

 Blame Angry

 Complain of Pain

 Talk to Adult

 Complain of Pain 2

Coping Cards 3

 Play

 Say Sorry

 Run Away

 Worry

 Stay Calm

Index

Note: References in *italics* are to figures.

3-year-old group modifications: animal totems 49; art/feeling faces 30; bucket filling 72; caring behaviours 52; caring for the environment 47; coping with feelings 40; cultural differences 68; feeling thermometer 38; feelings/facial expressions 25; kind acts 84; STOP/THINK/DO 77; voice levels 32; what feelings look like 33

active learning 2
Adderley, A. 6
art 18; animal totems 49; caring behaviours *50*, 50–52, *52*, *53*; caring poems 55; COPE-Resilience game 88; a day of feelings 38, *38*; feeling faces 30, *31*; friendly cards 71; handmade gifts for each other 53; hunting and gathering for pleasant feelings 86; sending caring messages around the world 87; silence and busyness 63; we share a life 78
attachment theory 6
attention holding 20

Baron-Cohen, S. 12
behaviour reinforcement 20
Bioecological Systems Theory 4, *5*
body, mindfulness of 99
Bowlby, John 6
Brackett, Marc 6, 7
Bronfenbrenner, Uri 2, 3–5
Bullied 64–65

CALD (culturally and linguistically diverse) 14
caring for others 22, 41; art 49–53, 55, 63; feelings explorer 41–42, 45, 46–47, 48; getting hurt 43–44; movement 54; role-play 60–61
caring/kindness 12

Cognitive Development Theory 2–3
cognitive empathy 13
Concrete Operational stage 2
considerations for educators/facilitators 16, 19; create a safe nurturing environment 19; "empathy" role model for children 19–20; encourage children to practice skills 20; holding children's attention 20–21; positive reinforcement 20; working with children with trauma 21
COPE-R: aims of the program 11; development of the program 13–14; introduction 11; program background 11; program in brief 16, *17*; Taiwanese adaptation 14; theoretical basis for topic areas 12–13
coping: images 102–103; research 9; resilience 9–10, 93; *see also* Early Years Coping Cards
cultural differences 67–68
culturally and linguistically diverse (CALD) 14

Early Years Coping Cards 9, 13, 17, 18, 102–103; *see also* situation and coping images
Early Years Situation Cards 9; Bullied 64–65; Choosing a Group to Play With *73*, 73–74; Getting Hurt 43–44; Wanting to Play with others 56–57, *57*; *see also* situation and coping images
Ecological Systems Theory 2, 3–5, *4*
emotional empathy 13
emotional intelligence (EI) 6–7
emotional literacy 7
emotional self-regulation 6
emotional understanding (EU) 12, 17
empathic sharing 13, 23, 73; art 78; choosing a group to play with *73*, 73–74; creating a sharing poem/song 79;

Index

feelings explorer 75, 80, 81; movement 79; role-play 76–77, 85
empathy 12, 13; facial expressions 92; role model for children 19–20
environment 19, 46–47

facial expressions 30, *31*, 92
Feelings Explorers 18; caring for animals 48; caring for the environment 46–47; The Caring Tree 83; coping with feelings 39–40; cultural differences 67–68; finding feelings 24–26, *26*; helping others feel better 81; how a good listener listens 58, *59*; how are you feeling? 45; how can we share 75; I'm happy to help 66; kind acts 84; noticing feelings in others 27–28; pick a feeling 29; quiet spaces 35; understanding others 80; voice chart 32; what is caring? 41–42
Formal Operations 2
foundation skills: understanding emotions 22, 24; art 30, *31*, 38; feelings explorer 24–29, 32, 35, 39; movement 37, *37*; role play 33, *34*, 36
foundations of COPE-R: outline 11; research overview 9–10; theoretical basis for topic areas 12–14; theoretical concepts 2–8

Goleman, Daniel 6

helping 66
holistic well-being 8
hurt 43–44

icons 16, 17, 18
implementation: considerations for educators/facilitators 16, 19–21; icon legends 16, 17, 18; program activities 16, 22–23; program in brief 16, 17; supplementary materials 16, 95; teacher's experience and reflection 16, 94

kindness 12, 84; *see also* caring for others

listening 58, *59*

Mayer, J. D. 6
mindfulness of senses, body and self 99
movement 18; bucket filling 72; creating a mandala of silence 89–91, *90*, *91*; creating a sharing poem/song 79; dance our feelings 37, *37*; looking after ourselves too 54; types of communication 62

open communication 12–13, 56, *57*; art 63; feelings explorer 58, *59*; movement 62; role-play 60–61; wanting to play with others 56–57, *57*

Petersen, L. 6
Piaget, Jean 2–3
poetry 18, *34*, 55, 79
politeness 13, 23, 64; art 71; Bullied 64–65; feelings explorers 66–68; movement 72; role-play 69–70
Positive Education in the pre-school years 7–8
positive psychology 7
positive reinforcement for appropriate behaviours 20
Pre-Operational stage 2
Process-Person-Context-Time (PPCT) model 5
program activities 16, 17, 56–63; foundation skills: understanding emotions 12, 22, 24–40; Topic 1: caring for others 12, 22, 41–63; Topic 2: open communication 12–13, 22, 56–63; Topic 3: politeness 13, 23, 64–72; Topic 4: empathic sharing 13, 23, 73–82, 85; Topic 5: review 23, 82–93
program in brief 16, 17

quiet spaces 35

relaxation 100
resilience 9–10, 93
review: art 86–88; feelings explorers 83–84; mix and match: facial expressions 92; movement 89–91; overview 82; rites of passage: training resilience 93; role-play 85
role-play 18; guess the emotion 36; polite behaviours 69–70; sharing from one teapot 85; supportive statements 60–61; tricky sharing situations 76–77; what feelings look like 33, *34*
RULER program 6, 7

safe nurturing environment 19
Salovey, P. 6

Index

scaffolding 3
schema 2
self, mindfulness of 99
self-regulation 6
Seligman, M. E. P. et al. 7
senses, mindfulness of 99
Sensorimotor stage 2
sharing *see* empathic sharing
situation and coping images 101–103
Smith, C. A. 12
social intelligence 7
social skills 7, 20
Socio-Cultural Theory of Development 3
songs 18, 37, 79, 82
supplementary materials 16, 95

Taiwanese adaptation of the COPE-R program 14
teacher's experience and reflection 16, 94
Teaching Tips 18
theoretical basis for topic areas in COPE-R 12–14
theoretical concepts underpinning COPE-R 2, *4*; attachment theory 6; Ecological Systems Theory 2, 3–5, *4*; emotional intelligence 6–7; Positive Education in the pre-school years 7–8; positive psychology 7; Process-Person-Context-Time (PPCT) model 5; self-regulation 6; Socio-Cultural Theory of Development 3, *4*; Theory of Cognitive Development 2–3, *4*
Theory of Cognitive Development 2–3, *4*
Theory of Mind (ToM) 12
topic activities 17
topic areas: 1: caring for others 41–55; 2: open communication 56–63; 3: politeness 64–72; 4: empathic sharing 73–81; 5: review 82–93; theoretical basis 12–14
traumatic events 21

voice chart 32
Vygotsky, Lev 2, 3

wanting to play *57*
wanting to play with others 56–57
Wheelwright, S. 12
Wu, M. Y. *et al.* 14

zone of proximal development (ZPD) 3